Academic Encounters

2nd Edition

Kim Sanabria
Carlos Sanabria
Series Editor: Bernard Seal

LISTENING

SPEAKING

2

CAMBRIDGE
UNIVERSITY PRESS

CAMBRIDGE
UNIVERSITY PRESS

University Printing House, Cambridge CB2 8BS, United Kingdom

One Liberty Plaza, 20th Floor, New York, NY 10006, USA

477 Williamstown Road, Port Melbourne, VIC 3207, Australia

314–321, 3rd Floor, Plot 3, Splendor Forum, Jasola District Centre, New Delhi – 110025, India

79 Anson Road, #06–04/06, Singapore 079906

Cambridge University Press is part of the University of Cambridge.

It furthers the University's mission by disseminating knowledge in the pursuit of education, learning and research at the highest international levels of excellence.

www.cambridge.org
Information on this title: www.cambridge.org/9781108638722

First published 2007
Second edition 2013

20 19 18 17 16 15 14 13 12 11 10 9 8 7 6 5

Printed in Mexico by Editorial Impresora Apolo, S.A. de C.V.

A catalogue record for this publication is available from the British Library

Library of Congress Cataloging in Publication Data

Sanabria, Kim, 1955-
Academic encounters : American studies : listening, speaking / Kim Sanabria, Carlos Sanabria. — Second edition.
pages cm. — (Academic encounters)
Includes index.
ISBN 978-1-107-65516-4 (pbk. : level 2) — ISBN 978-1-107-63266-0 (audio : level 2)
1. English language—Textbooks for foreign speakers. 2. English language—Rhetoric—Problems, exercises, etc. 3. Listening—Problems, exercises, etc. 4. Study skills—Problems, exercises, etc. 5. United States—Civilization—Problems, exercises, etc. 6. Readers—United States. I. Sanabria, Carlos, 1950- II. Title.

PE1128.S23 2013
428.2'4—dc23

2013004916

ISBN 978-1-108-63872-2 Student's Book with Integrated Digital Learning
ISBN 978-1-107-68883-4 Teacher's Manual

Additional resources for this publication at www.cambridge.org/academicencounters

Art direction and layout services: Kamae Design, Oxford, UK
Photo research: Suzanne Williams
Audio production: John Marshall Media
Video production: Steadman Productions

Table of Contents

Scope and Sequence

V Vocabulary Skills	**N** Note Taking Skills	Learning Outcomes
Reading and thinking about the topic Building background knowledge on the topic Building background knowledge and vocabulary Examining vocabulary in context Guessing vocabulary from context	Using information the lecturer puts on the board Taking good lecture notes	Prepare and deliver an oral presentation on an American president
Reading and thinking about the topic Examining vocabulary in context Guessing vocabulary from context	Understanding numbers, dates, and time expressions Using symbols and abbreviations Using a map to organize your notes Conducting a survey	

V Vocabulary Skills	**N** Note Taking Skills	Learning Outcomes
Reading and thinking about the topic Building background knowledge on the topic Examining vocabulary in context Guessing vocabulary from context	Taking notes on handouts Organizing your notes in columns	Prepare and deliver an oral presentation in pairs on an interview conducted outside of class
Reading and thinking about the topic Building background knowledge on the topic Examining vocabulary in context Guessing vocabulary from context	Reviewing and revising notes Using bullets to organize your notes	

Unit 3: The Struggle for Equality • 83

Unit 4: American Values • 125

V Vocabulary Skills	**N** Note Taking Skills	Learning Outcomes
Reading and thinking about the topic Building background knowledge on the topic Examining vocabulary in context Guessing vocabulary from context	Creating your own symbols and abbreviations Organizing your notes in a chart	Prepare and deliver a poster presentation on an individual who played a role in the struggle for equality
Reading and thinking about the topic Building background knowledge on the topic Examining vocabulary in context Guessing vocabulary from context	Understanding numbers, dates, and time expressions Using symbols and abbreviations Using a map to organize your notes Indenting Using an outline Using your notes to make a time line Conducting a survey	

V Vocabulary Skills	**N** Note Taking Skills	Learning Outcomes
Reading and thinking about the topic Building background knowledge on the topic Examining vocabulary in context Guessing vocabulary from context	Clarifying your notes Taking notes on questions and answers	Prepare and deliver an oral presentation on a value you consider important
Reading and thinking about the topic Examining vocabulary in context Building background knowledge on the topic Guessing vocabulary from context	Taking notes in a point-by-point format Using information on the board to help you take notes	

Academic Encounters:
Academic Preparation Through Sustained Content

The Series

Academic Encounters is a sustained content-based series for English language learners preparing to study college-level subject matter in English. The goal of the series is to expose students to the types of texts and tasks that they will encounter in their academic course work and provide them with the skills to be successful when that encounter occurs.

Academic Content

At each level in the series, there are two thematically paired books. One is an academic reading and writing skills book, in which students encounter readings that are based on authentic academic texts. In this book, students are given the skills to understand texts and respond to them in writing. The reading and writing book is paired with an academic listening and speaking skills book, in which students encounter discussion and lecture material specially prepared by experts in their field. In this book, students learn how to take notes from a lecture, participate in discussions, and prepare short presentations.

Flexibility

The books at each level may be used as stand-alone reading and writing books or listening and speaking books. They may also be used together to create a complete four-skills course. This is made possible because the content of each book at each level is very closely related. Each unit and chapter, for example, has the same title and deals with similar content, so that teachers can easily focus on different skills, but the same content, as they toggle from one book to the other. Additionally, if the books are taught together, when students are presented with the culminating unit writing or speaking assignment, they will have a rich and varied supply of reading and lecture material to draw on.

A Sustained Content Approach

A sustained content approach teaches language through the study of subject matter from one or two related academic content areas. This approach simulates the experience of university courses and better prepares students for academic study.

Students benefit from a sustained content approach

Real-world academic language and skills

Students learn how to understand and use academic language because they are studying actual academic content.

An authentic, intensive experience

By immersing students in the language of a single academic discipline, sustained content helps prepare them for the rigor of later coursework.

Natural recycling of language

Because a sustained content course focuses on a particular academic discipline, concepts and language recur. As students progress through the course, their ability to work with authentic language improves dramatically.

Knowledge of common academic content

When students work with content from the most popular university courses, they gain real knowledge of these academic disciplines. This helps them to be more successful when they move on to later coursework.

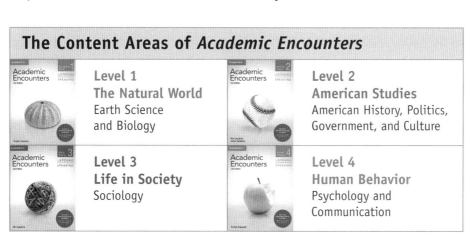

The Content Areas of *Academic Encounters*

Level 1 **The Natural World** Earth Science and Biology	**Level 2** **American Studies** American History, Politics, Government, and Culture
Level 3 **Life in Society** Sociology	**Level 4** **Human Behavior** Psychology and Communication

Academic Skills

Academic Encounters, Listening and Speaking teaches skills in 4 main areas. A set of icons highlights which skills are practiced in each exercise.

 Listening Skills

The listening skills tasks are designed to help students develop strategies before listening, while listening, and after listening.

 Speaking Skills

Students learn how to participate in formal and informal situations at universities, including sharing opinions, presenting research, and creating extended oral presentations. These skills and tasks were carefully selected to prepare students for university study.

 Vocabulary Skills

Vocabulary learning is an essential part of academic preparation. Tasks throughout the books focus on particular sets of vocabulary that are important for reading in a particular subject area as well as vocabulary from the Academic Word List.

 Note Taking Skills

In order to succeed in university courses, students need to be able to take notes effectively. Each unit teaches a range of note taking skills, ranging from organizational strategies and listening for key numbers to using your notes to prepare for tests.

Preparing for
Authentic Listening

3 Listening for numerical information L N S

Listening for numbers and dates can be very difficult in a second language. Here are some suggestions to help you understand numerical information about history.

1. Learn the words and phrases often used to refer to time periods.

century = 100 years   *decade* = 10 years
twentieth century = 1900–1999   *figure* = number
the mid-1930s = around 1935   *the early 1940s* = 1940–1943

2. Learn verbs that often describe numbers.

go up = increase, rise, climb
go down = decrease, fall, decline

A Work with a partner and look at the graph below. It shows legal immigration to the United States from 1820 to 2010 according to the U.S. Census Bureau.

◄)) **B** Listen to a description of immigration patterns to the United States. Fill in the missing parts of the graph with the information you hear.

Source: U.S. Census Bureau: Statistical Yearbook Bureau of Citizenship and Immigration Services

C Work with a partner and compare answers. Then discuss this question: What is the main difference between immigration patterns to the United States in the nineteenth and the twentieth centuries?

Chapter 3 *The Origins of Diver*

Students develop a range of **skills** to help them **anticipate and prepare** for the listening tasks.

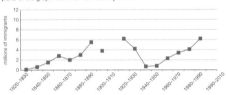

INTERVIEW 1   Reasons for Voting or Not Voting

1 Examining vocabulary in context V

Here are some words and phrases from the interview with Manuel, Mary, Kelly, and Ralph, printed in **bold** and given in the context in which you will hear them. They are followed by definitions.

It's still not **convenient** for a lot of people: *easy to do*
I just **couldn't make it**: *couldn't go somewhere as planned*
You know, voting gives you **a voice**: *an opportunity to express yourself*
When you vote, you get to say . . . who can help more in **dealing with** the country's problems: *trying to solve*
I think voting is a **civic duty**: *a responsibility of a citizen*
I read that in 34 countries, voting is **an obligation**: *something you must do*
Actually, I don't **trust** most politicians: *believe in*

2 Listening for different ways of saying *yes* and *no* L S

Speakers don't always answer *Yes / No* questions with those exact words. Here are some other ways of saying *yes* and *no*.

Yes	No
Sure.	I would have, but . . .
Definitely.	Well, not usually.
Of course (I do)!	Of course not!
Absolutely.	Not really.
Yeah. (informal)	Nope. / Nah. (informal)

◄)) **A** Listen to the interview. The interviewer asks four people if they vote. Do they answer *yes* or *no*? Match the speakers with their reasons.

_____ 1. Manuel   a. Yes, because voting gives you a voice.
_____ 2. Mary   b. No, because there is no holiday on Election Day.
_____ 3. Kelly   c. No, because you can't trust most politicians.
_____ 4. Ralph   d. Yes, because voting is a civic duty.

B Work with a partner and compare answers. Then discuss whether you agree or disagree with the reasons the speakers give for voting or not voting.

The first listenings are **authentic interviews,** in which students develop **skills such as listening for main ideas and details.**

8 Unit 1 *Laws of the Land*

Academic Listening and Speaking

Understanding humor about the topic ⑤

Many jokes and cartoons play with words and their meanings – they use common words and phrases in unexpected ways. Being able to appreciate humor shows that you understand a language on different levels.

A Look at the cartoon and read the caption.

"The way I see it, the Constitution cuts both ways. The First Amendment gives you the right to say what you want, but the Second Amendment gives me the right to shoot you for it."

B Work with a partner or a small group and answer the following questions.

1. Where are the people in the cartoon? What are they doing?
2. What does the speaker mean when he says the Constitution "cuts both ways"?
3. Is the speaker's description of the First and Second Amendments correct?
4. Is the speaker serious? How do you know?
5. Do you think the cartoon is funny? Why or why not?

Chapter 2 *Constitutional Issues Tod*

Post-listening activities help students **analyze and understand** the authentic inverviews.

---

3 In Your Own Voice

In this section, you will practice asking and answering questions about the United States. Form two groups. Group A, follow the directions below. Group B, go to the next page and follow the directions there.

Asking and answering questions: Group A ⑤

A Read the information below. You will need to tell other students about what you have read, so make sure you understand it and can pronounce all the words clearly.

U.S. national holidays: Thanksgiving, Independence Day (the Fourth of July), Memorial Day, Labor Day, Veterans Day

The founding fathers: George Washington, Benjamin Franklin, John Adams, Thomas Jefferson, James Madison, Alexander Hamilton

Recent U.S. government leaders: William Clinton, Hillary Rodham Clinton, George W. Bush, Barack Obama

First Ladies: Michelle Obama, Laura Bush, Hillary Rodham Clinton, Barbara Bush, Nancy Reagan, Betty Ford

The American flag: The U.S. flag has 50 stars and 13 stripes.

The American Constitution: The Constitution was adopted in 1789.

B Next, look at the grid and try to answer the questions.

1. Can you name the capital of the United States?	2. Do you know the number of states in the United States today?	3. Do you know the name of the national anthem (national song)?
4. Can you tell me what the colors of the American flag symbolize?	5. Do you know when America declared its independence?	6. Do you know where the U.S. president lives?

C Now work with a partner from Group B. Take turns asking your partner the questions in the grid, in whatever order you like. (Group B has different questions to ask.) When your partner asks you a question, listen carefully. Then use the information you read in Step A to answer the questions.

D Listen carefully to the response that Student B gives you. Try to repeat it.

Example:

Oh, I see. So the capital of the United States is Washington, D.C.

Students then study and practice using discrete **speaking skills**, as they express their own opinions about the **academic content**.

Academic Lectures and Note Taking

4 Academic Listening and Note Taking

In this section, you will hear and take notes on a two-part lecture given by David Chachere, a lecturer on political science. The title of his lecture is "Two Important Laws in the Struggle for Equality."

BEFORE THE LECTURE

1 Sharing your opinion ⓢ

Look at the photographs below and discuss the following questions with a partner:

1. What do the people in the photographs have in common?
2. What difficulties do these people probably face?
3. How could laws help these people to participate fully in society?

Student

Woodworker

Office worker

Athlete

114 Unit 3 *The Struggle for*

> The full-color **design mirrors university textbooks**, providing students with an **authentic university experience**.

> Each unit provides extensive instruction and practice in **taking notes**, helping **students succeed** in university courses.

B Read the incomplete notes from Part 1 of Professor Smith's lecture on the civil rights movement. Notice that the note taker used columns to record the guiding questions and matching answers. Predict the kind of information you need to listen for to complete the notes.

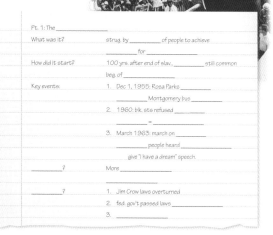

```
Pt. 1: The _____
What was it?          strug. by _____ of people to achieve
                      _____ for _____
How did it start?     100 yrs. after end of slav., _____ still common
                      beg. of _____
Key events:           1.  Dec 1, 1955: Rosa Parks _____
                          _____ Montgomery bus _____
                      2.  1960: blk. sts refused _____
                          _____ = _____
                      3.  March 1963: march on _____
                          _____ people heard _____
                          give "I have a dream" speech.
_____ ?          More _____
                      _____
_____ ?          1.  Jim Crow laws overturned
                      2.  fed. gov't passed laws _____
                      3.  _____
```

🔊 **C** Now watch or listen to Part 1 of the lecture and complete the notes. Include your
👥 symbols and abbreviations from Step A.

D Work with a partner and compare notes. Then use them to review the guiding questions and matching answers.

98 Unit 3 *The Struggle for Equality*

> Academic lectures take place in real college classrooms, complete with interactions between professors and students.

Academic Vocabulary and Oral Presentations

Unit 1 Academic Vocabulary Review

This section reviews the vocabulary from Chapters 1 and 2. Some of the words you needed to learn to understand the content of this unit are specific to its topics. Other words are more general. They appear across different academic fields and are extremely useful for all students to know. For a complete list of all the Academic Word List words in this book, see the Appendix on page 182.

A Read the news articles. The boxes include pairs of related words. Choose the correct word from each pair to complete the sentences. You will not use all of the words.

Worried About Nature?

A large public (1) _____ recently showed that (2) _____ pollution is a worry to many people, but finding solutions that work is a big (3) _____ . Recently, the government (4) _____ a new study to research ways that companies could reduce pollution. The study was (5) _____ , but it suggested that companies must take more responsibility for protecting the environment. However, companies said that the proposed solutions were too expensive and criticized the press for overreacting.

> authority, authorized
> challenge, challenging
> conclusion, inconclusive
> demonstration, demonstrate
> environment, environmental

Are the Police Doing Their Job?

The issue of privacy has become increasingly (6) _____ in recent years. In the Constitution, the (7) _____ fathers laid the basis for the right to privacy. However, this right is difficult to (8) _____ correctly. Some people think the police should be able to ask for a person's (9) _____ if that person is acting in a suspicious way. Others, however, say that is probably unconstitutional and (10) _____ .

> controversy, controversial
> foundation, founding
> identification, unidentified
> interpretation, interpret
> legality, illegal

Banned from Sports?

For many Muslim women, the headscarf (11) _____ their religious beliefs. One woman, Shariqua Jones, said that for her and her family, wearing the scarf was not a (12) _____ but a matter of personal choice. However, when her daughter wanted to (13) _____ in a sports event, she was asked to remove her scarf. Ms. Jones said that this was not fair. She remarked: "(14) _____ , school officials are not taking this issue seriously enough. Everyone should be treated (15) _____ . My daughter has the same rights as other children."

> obvious, obviously
> participation, participate
> requirement, required
> similarity, similarly
> symbol, symbolizes

Chapter 2 Academic Vocabulary Review

Academic vocabulary development is **critical to student success.** Each unit includes **intensive vocabulary practice**, including words from the Academic Word List.

Students create **oral presentations,** applying the vocabulary and academic content they study in each unit, and **preparing them to speak in a university classroom.**

Oral Presentation

In groups, you will research an individual who represents the struggle for equality in the United States. Then you will make a poster about this person and present it to the class.

BEFORE THE PRESENTATION

A Work with a small group of two to three people. Choose a person to research from the list below.

Susan B. Anthony	Abraham Lincoln	Rosa Parks
George Washington Carver	Martin Luther King Jr.	Paul Robeson
César Chávez	Lucretia Mott	Sonia Sotomayor
Frederick Douglass	Barack Obama	Elizabeth Cady Stanton
Betty Friedan	Jackie Robinson	Other (your own choice)

B Make a poster that illustrates what you find (an example appears below). Include photos or pictures and details about the person's:

- date and place of birth and/or death
- achievements and struggle for equality
- most important contributions to society
- other interesting information

Dates and Details About George Washington Carver

He was born into slavery around 1864 (exact date unknown).
After slavery was abolished, his former master, Moses Carver, raised him as his own child.
He died in 1943.

Profession
Scientist (botanist), educator, and inventor

Education and Achievements
As a young child, Carver had to move 10 miles from his home to attend a school that admitted black children. When he was older, he was rejected from college because of his race. However, he was eventually accepted at another college, became the first black student there, and after he graduated, became the first black professor at the college. Later on in life, as a professional, Carver achieved national recognition for his work.

Significance
Carver was inspired by this advice from a woman who helped him go to school:
"You must learn all you can, then go back out into the world and give your learning back to the people."
He believed passionately in social harmony, although he saw a lot of injustice in his life, including the effects of segregation and extreme violence against blacks.
As a scientist and educator, Carver used his skills to improve the quality of life of poor black farmers in the South. He promoted the cultivation of peanuts and sweet potatoes instead of cotton. His work in crop rotation led to important progress in agriculture and nutrition for millions of people, black and white.
On his grave, it says:
"He could have added fortune to fame, but caring for neither, he found happiness and honor in being helpful to the world."

To the student

Welcome to *Academic Encounters 2 Listening and Speaking: American Studies!*

The *Academic Encounters* series gets its name because in this series you will *encounter*, or meet, the kinds of *academic* texts (lectures and readings), *academic* language (grammar and vocabulary), and *academic* tasks (taking tests, writing papers, and giving presentations) that you will encounter when you study an academic subject area in English. The goal of the series, therefore, is to prepare you for that encounter.

The approach of *Academic Encounters 2 Listening and Speaking: American Studies*, may be different from what you are used to in your English studies. In this book, you are asked to study an academic subject area and be responsible for learning that information, in the same way as you might study in a college or university course. You will find that as you study this information, you will at the same time improve your English language proficiency and develop the skills that you will need to be successful when you come to study in your own academic subject area in English.

In *Academic Encounters 2 Listening and Speaking: American Studies* for example, you will learn:

- what to listen for in academic lectures
- how to think critically about what you have heard
- how to participate in conversations and more formal discussions
- how to give oral presentations in an academic style
- methods of preparing for tests
- strategies for dealing with new vocabulary
- note-taking and study techniques

This course is designed to help you study in English in *any* subject matter. However, because during the study of this book, you will learn a lot of new information about research findings and theories in the field of sociology, you may feel that by the end you have enough background information to one day take and be successful in an introductory course in sociology in English.

We certainly hope that you find *Academic Encounters 2 Listening and Speaking: American Studies* useful. We also hope that you will find it to be enjoyable. It is important to remember that the most successful learning takes place when you enjoy what you are studying and find it interesting.

Author's acknowledgments

We would like to express our gratitude to many individuals whose support and guidance have been invaluable as we worked on Academic Encounters 2, Listening and Speaking: American Studies.

Bernard Seal, as series editor, deserves great praise for conceptualizing and overseeing the project. On a weekly basis, we have worked with Christopher Sol Cruz, editorial manager and a trusted source of balance and insight. We also thank Michael Ryall, our development editor, who helped us examine each page. Finally, Kathleen O'Reilly, who worked with us on the first edition, has often been foremost in our thoughts.

Many other individuals have contributed to the Academic Encounters series, notably Caitlin Mara, Managing Editor, Sheryl Olinsky Borg, Publishing Manager, and the design, audio, and video producers. It goes without saying large projects depend on the attentive talents of dedicated professionals like these, and we are especially grateful to them.

Finally, to the interviewees and lecturers who have added depth and authenticity to our efforts, we extend our most sincere appreciation.

Carlos Sanabria and Kim Sanabria

Publisher's acknowledgments

The first edition of *Academic Encounters* has been used by many teachers in many institutions all around the world. Over the years, countless instructors have passed on feedback about the series, all of which has proven invaluable in helping to direct the vision for the second edition. More formally, a number of reviewers also provided us with a detailed analysis of the series, and we are especially grateful for their insights. We would therefore like to extend particular thanks to the following instructors:

Pamela Guntharp Dzunu, Washington University in St. Louis, St. Louis, Missouri
Anne Lech, Northwest Missouri State University, Maryville, Missouri
John Stasinopoulos, College of DuPage, Glen Ellyn, Illinois
Roberta Steinberg, Mount Ida College, Newton, Massachusetts

Unit 1
Laws of the Land

The Adoption of the Constitution, J. B. Stearns

In this unit, you will learn about the U.S. Constitution, the document that is the basis for the structure of the government of the United States. Chapter 1 focuses on the basic organization of the government and the history behind it. You will hear people of various ages and backgrounds speaking about why they do or do not vote, and you will hear a lecture about the three branches of the U.S. government. In Chapter 2, you will learn about the Bill of Rights, which are the first 10 amendments, or changes, to the Constitution. The interviews in Chapter 2 are about topics in the Constitution that often create disagreement among Americans. The lecture discusses freedom of speech.

Contents

In Unit 1, you will listen to and speak about the following topics.

Chapter 1 The Foundations of Government	Chapter 2 Constitutional Issues Today
Interview 1 Reasons for Voting or Not Voting **Interview 2** Voter Turnout **Lecture** The Structure of the U.S. Federal Government	**Interview 1** Important Constitutional Rights **Interview 2** A Controversial Right **Lecture** The First Amendment

Skills

In Unit 1, you will practice the following skills.

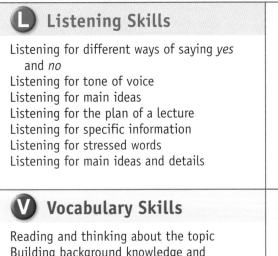 **Listening Skills**

Listening for different ways of saying *yes* and *no*
Listening for tone of voice
Listening for main ideas
Listening for the plan of a lecture
Listening for specific information
Listening for stressed words
Listening for main ideas and details

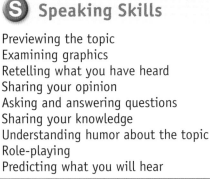 **Speaking Skills**

Previewing the topic
Examining graphics
Retelling what you have heard
Sharing your opinion
Asking and answering questions
Sharing your knowledge
Understanding humor about the topic
Role-playing
Predicting what you will hear

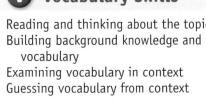 **Vocabulary Skills**

Reading and thinking about the topic
Building background knowledge and vocabulary
Examining vocabulary in context
Guessing vocabulary from context

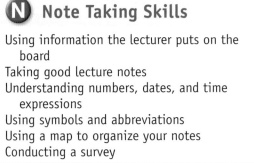 **Note Taking Skills**

Using information the lecturer puts on the board
Taking good lecture notes
Understanding numbers, dates, and time expressions
Using symbols and abbreviations
Using a map to organize your notes
Conducting a survey

Learning Outcomes

Prepare and **deliver** an oral presentation on an American president

Chapter 1
The Foundations of Government

The Great Seal of the United States

1 Getting Started

In this section, you will read about the foundations, or beginnings, of the United States government. You will also listen to a conversation about some important symbols that are found on the Great Seal of the United States. The seal is used on passports and other official government documents.

1 Reading and thinking about the topic

Reading and thinking about a topic before you hear about it helps you to review what you already know and to get ready to listen to new information.

A Read the following passage.

The United States has had its system of government for more than 200 years. This system is based on a number of important principles.

First, the United States is a *republic*. This means that the head of the government is a president, not a king or queen. Second, the United States is a *democracy*. In other words, representatives chosen by the people have the power to make decisions. Citizens of the United States have the right to vote for their president and other representatives in regular, free elections. *Federalism* is another important principle. It means that there are different levels of government: the federal (national) level, the state level, and the local level.

According to the Constitution, the federal government has three branches: the legislative branch (Congress); the executive branch (the president and vice president); and the judicial branch (the court system). Under a system of *checks and balances*, each branch has separate responsibilities, but the branches work together to govern the country. The men who wrote the Constitution designed the government this way so that no branch would have too much power.

B Answer the following questions according to the information in the passage.

    1. What are three principles that form the foundation of the U.S. government?

    2. What is one important right that U.S. citizens have?

    3. What is the purpose of the system of checks and balances?

C Read these questions and share your responses with a partner.

    1. How is the U.S. government similar to or different from other governments that you know about?

    2. In the United States, people vote for their president and representatives. How are leaders chosen in other countries you know about?

2 Building background knowledge on the topic Ⓥ Ⓢ

A The American flag is one of the most important symbols of the country. Read the statements and guess whether they are *T* (true) or *F* (false). Share your guesses with a partner. Then look at the answer key on the next page.

  _____ **1.** The flag is usually displayed from sunrise to sunset.

  _____ **2.** The flag can only be displayed on national holidays.

  _____ **3.** When it is carried, the flag should be held flat, or horizontal.

  _____ **4.** The flag flies at half-mast (halfway up) when the country has experienced a loss.

  _____ **5.** American citizens are required to salute the flag during ceremonies.

  _____ **6.** The flag should never be allowed to touch the floor.

  _____ **7.** Folding the flag indicates extreme danger.

  _____ **8.** Very old flags should be disposed of by burning them.

  _____ **9.** The flag should be folded in quarters to be put away.

  _____ **10.** The flag is never used on postage stamps.

B The answers for "Building background knowledge on the topic" are at the bottom of this page. Look at the answers and then discuss the following questions.

1. Did any of the answers surprise you? Why?

2. What do you think are the reasons for these customs?

3 Previewing the topic Ⓢ Ⓛ

Previewing means looking at pictures or other visual materials, skimming handouts that your teacher gives you, or perhaps reviewing key vocabulary about a topic before listening to people talk about it. Doing these things will prepare you for listening and will improve your ability to understand what you hear.

A You will hear a conversation about some symbols that appear on the back of a U.S. one-dollar bill. Look at the numbered symbols in this picture. Find the same symbols in the larger picture on page 3. What are they? Can you guess what each symbol represents?

B Now listen to the conversation and write the number of each symbol next to what it represents in the list below.

_____ **a.** The national symbol of the United States

_____ **b.** The 13 original states of the United States

_____ **c.** The fact that America is a country with a strong foundation

_____ **d.** The fact that the United States is one nation made of many states and many people

_____ **e.** The year that the United States became independent from Britain

1. T, 2. F, 3. F, 4. T, 5. F, 6. T, 7. F, 8. T, 9. F, 10. F
Answers to "Building background knowledge on the topic," page 4

Chapter 1 *The Foundations of Government* **5**

2 Real-Life Voices

In this section, you will hear five people of different ages and backgrounds talk about voting. First you will hear Manuel, Mary, Kelly, and Ralph discuss why they do or do not vote. Then you will hear Robert talking about voter turnout (the percentage of eligible voters who vote in an election).

BEFORE THE INTERVIEWS

1 Building background knowledge and vocabulary Ⓥ Ⓢ

> Learning background information and vocabulary related to a topic can help you understand the topic better when you listen to people talking about it.

Americans voting on Election Day

A The following words and expressions are used to talk about voting. Work in a small group and match the words with their meanings. Check your answers in a dictionary if necessary.

1. candidate	_____	**a.** to compete for votes
2. compulsory	_____	**b.** a person who is nominated for an election
3. election	_____	**c.** required or obligatory
4. go to the polls	_____	**d.** to go to a voting station
5. issue	_____	**e.** an important topic
6. party	_____	**f.** a political group
7. run for office	_____	**g.** the process of choosing a government representative

B Form a group. Read this passage about voting in the United States. Use vocabulary from Step A to fill in the blanks. You may have to change the form of a noun or verb. Then check your answers with the members of your group.

All U.S. citizens have the right to vote in national (1) _____ at the age of 18. Voting is also called (2) "_____ ." In the United States, voting is voluntary, not (3) _____ . Voters choose the (4) _____ they support and vote for that person on Election Day.

Voters may make their decision for different reasons. One reason might be that they support a particular (5) _____ (Democratic, Republican, etc.). Another reason might be that they feel strongly about a particular (6) _____ , such as the economy, crime, or freedom of expression, and they want to express their opinion by electing the candidate who agrees with them.

In most cases, there are only two candidates in a U.S. election: a Democrat and a Republican. Sometimes, a third candidate may (7) _____ , but third-party candidates almost never win in the United States.

2 Examining graphics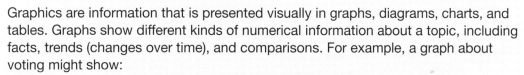

Graphics are information that is presented visually in graphs, diagrams, charts, and tables. Graphs show different kinds of numerical information about a topic, including facts, trends (changes over time), and comparisons. For example, a graph about voting might show:

> **a fact:** the number of people or percentage of the population that votes
> **a trend:** an increase or decrease in the number of people who vote
> **a comparison:** the difference in voting practices between one year and another

The graph shows voter turnout between 1940 and 2012. Work with a partner and study the graph. Then discuss the questions that follow.

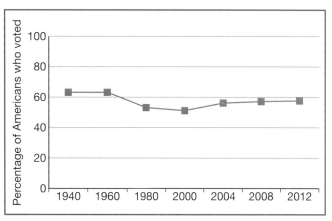

Source: Federal Election Commission

1. Does this graph show some facts, a trend, a comparison, or all of these? Explain your answer.
2. In what years was voter turnout the highest?
3. What happened between 1960 and 1980?
4. Approximately what percentage of people voted in 2008 and 2012?
5. Does any information in the graph surprise you? Why or why not?

1 Examining vocabulary in context ⓥ

Here are some words and phrases from the interview with Manuel, Mary, Kelly, and Ralph, printed in **bold** and given in the context in which you will hear them. They are followed by definitions.

> It's still not **convenient** for a lot of people: *easy to do*
>
> I just **couldn't make it**: *couldn't go somewhere as planned*
>
> You know, voting gives you **a voice**: *an opportunity to express yourself*
>
> When you vote, you get to say . . . who can help more in **dealing with** the country's problems: *trying to solve*
>
> I think voting is a **civic duty**: *a responsibility of a citizen*
>
> I read that in 34 countries, voting is **an obligation**: *something you must do*
>
> Actually, I don't **trust** most politicians: *believe in*

2 Listening for different ways of saying *yes* and *no*

Speakers don't always answer *Yes / No* questions with those exact words. Here are some other ways of saying *yes* and *no*.

Yes	**No**
Sure.	*I would have, but . . .*
Definitely.	*Well, not usually.*
Of course (I do)!	*Of course not!*
Absolutely.	*Not really.*
Yeah. (informal)	*Nope. / Nah. (informal)*

🔊 **A** Listen to the interview. The interviewer asks four people if they vote. Do they answer *yes* or *no*? Match the speakers with their reasons.

_____ **1.** Manuel   **a.** Yes, because voting gives you a voice.

_____ **2.** Mary   **b.** No, because there is no holiday on Election Day.

_____ **3.** Kelly   **c.** No, because you can't trust most politicians.

_____ **4.** Ralph   **d.** Yes, because voting is a civic duty.

B Work with a partner and compare answers. Then discuss whether you agree or disagree with the reasons the speakers give for voting or not voting.

3 Listening for tone of voice 🅛

🔊 Listen again to excerpts from the interview. Circle the response that describes the speaker's tone. Compare answers with a partner.

Excerpt	Speaker	Tone of voice		
1	Manuel	unsure	enthusiastic	angry
2	Mary	afraid	certain	frustrated
3	Kelly	furious	excited	bored
4	Ralph	hopeless	interested	passionate

INTERVIEW 2 Voter Turnout

1 Examining vocabulary in context 🅥

Here are some words and phrases from the interview with Robert, printed in bold and given in the context in which you will hear them. They are followed by definitions.

Voting is becoming **increasingly** important: *more and more*

There are many problems that need to be **addressed**: *thought about, dealt with*

The environment is definitely a **critical** topic: *important*

Global warming is a huge problem, and we can't go on **ignoring** it: *paying no attention to*

Surely we have to make it a **priority** to get people back to work: *our main concern*

The political parties are **sharply** divided: *extremely*

2 Listening for main ideas 🅛 🅢

Main ideas are the important points that a speaker wants to make. In an interview, you have to listen carefully to the questions as well as the answers in order to understand the main ideas. For example:

Interviewer: *What problems are people concerned about?*
Robert: *Well, they're worried about things that affect them personally.*

One of Robert's main ideas is: People are worried about things that affect them personally.

A The following questions are about the main ideas in the interview with Robert. Read the questions before you listen.

1. Does Robert think that voting is important?

_____ **a.** Yes, he does.

_____ **b.** He's not sure.

_____ **c.** No, he doesn't.

2. Why does Robert think more people vote nowadays?

_____ **a.** Politicians are more popular than they used to be.

_____ **b.** Problems today are more serious than they were in the past.

_____ **c.** People are more aware of the issues today.

3. What is the most important issue, in Robert's opinion?

_____ **a.** crime

_____ **b.** the environment

_____ **c.** homelessness

4. Which other issues does Robert think are important? Check (✓) two issues.

_____ **a.** education

_____ **b.** equality

_____ **c.** the economy

_____ **d.** health care

_____ **e.** taxes

_____ **f.** immigration

B Now listen to the interview. Check (✓) all of Robert's responses to the questions.

C Work with a partner and compare answers. Then discuss the following question: Of the issues listed above, which ones are also important to you? Explain your response.

AFTER THE INTERVIEWS

1 Retelling what you have heard ⓢ

Using your own words to retell what you have heard is an important skill. It helps you check your understanding and review important ideas and vocabulary.

Work in groups of five students. Each member of the group should play the role of one of the speakers from the interviews (Manuel, Mary, Kelly, Ralph, or Robert). Take turns explaining why you do or do not vote. Ask each other questions about their reasons.

2 Sharing your opinion Ⓢ

Sharing opinions is a way to review material and learn about other people's ideas. You can use the following expressions to introduce your ideas.

I think . . .   *In my view, . . .*
I believe . . .   *I agree (with X) that . . .*
In my opinion, . . .   *I disagree (with Y) because . . .*

Work in small groups and discuss the ideas below. Use expressions from the box above to express your opinion and to respond to your classmates' opinions.

1. Do you agree or disagree with the following statements? Write "Agree" or "Disagree" in the spaces provided.

   _____ Voting should be compulsory.

   _____ Voting is a civic duty.

   _____ Election Day should be a national holiday.

   _____ Voting gives people power.

   _____ It does not make any difference whether you vote or not.

2. What are three goals that are important to you? Check (✓) the goals that you care about the most. Why do you care about them? In the space provided, write about another goal that matters to you.

   _____ Reducing the level of crime in society

   _____ Limiting air and water pollution

   _____ Making sure everyone has decent housing

   _____ Providing a good education to all children

   _____ Making sure all citizens are treated equally

   _____ Creating enough jobs

   _____ Making sure everyone has access to health care

   _____ Reducing taxes

   _____ Finding creative solutions to illegal immigration

   _____

3. Which characteristic do you think is most important in an elected representative? Choose a characteristic from the list below or add your own. Explain your responses.

   - honesty
   - good administrative skills
   - intelligence
   - love of one's country
   - good speaking skills
   - good looks
   - leadership skills
   - strong religious beliefs
   - _____
   - _____
   - _____
   - _____

3 In Your Own Voice

In this section, you will practice asking and answering questions about the United States. Form two groups. Group A, follow the directions below. Group B, go to the next page and follow the directions there.

Asking and answering questions: Group A ⓢ

A Read the information below. You will need to tell other students about what you have read, so make sure you understand it and can pronounce all the words clearly.

U.S. national holidays: Thanksgiving, Independence Day (the Fourth of July), Memorial Day, Labor Day, Veterans Day

The founding fathers: George Washington, Benjamin Franklin, John Adams, Thomas Jefferson, James Madison, Alexander Hamilton

Recent U.S. government leaders: William Clinton, Hillary Rodham Clinton, George W. Bush, Barack Obama

First Ladies: Michelle Obama, Laura Bush, Hillary Rodham Clinton, Barbara Bush, Nancy Reagan, Betty Ford

The American flag: The U.S. flag has 50 stars and 13 stripes.

The American Constitution: The Constitution was adopted in 1789.

B Next, look at the grid and try to answer the questions. Practice reading the questions aloud.

1. Can you name the capital of the United States?	2. Do you know the number of states in the United States today?	3. Do you know the name of the national anthem (national song)?
4. Can you tell me what the colors of the American flag symbolize?	5. Do you know when America declared its independence?	6. Do you know where the U.S. president lives?

C Now work with a partner from Group B. Take turns asking your partner the questions in the grid, in whatever order you like. (Group B has different questions to ask.) When your partner asks you a question, listen carefully. Then use the information you read in Step A to answer the questions.

D Listen carefully to the response that Student B gives you. Try to repeat it.

Example:

Oh, I see. So the capital of the United States is Washington, D.C.

Asking and answering questions: Group B ⓢ

A Read the information below. You will need to tell other students about what you have read, so make sure you understand it and can pronounce all the words clearly.

The capital of the United States: Washington, D.C.

Number of states in the Union: There are 50 states in the United States today.

National anthem: "The Star-Spangled Banner"

Colors of the American flag: Red represents bravery, white represents innocence and freedom, and blue represents justice.

Independence Day: America declared its independence on July 4, 1776.

Residence of the president: The president lives in the White House, Washington, D.C.

B Next, look at the grid and try to answer the questions. Practice reading the questions aloud.

1. Can you name two U.S. national holidays (not religious holidays)?	2. Can you name one of the founding fathers (eighteenth-century leaders) of the United States?	3. Can you name three current or recent U.S. government leaders?
4. Can you name two first ladies (presidents' wives)?	5. Can you tell me the pattern on the American flag?	6. Can you tell me when the Constitution was adopted?

C Now work with a partner from Group A. Take turns asking your partner the questions in the grid, in whatever order you like. (Group A has different questions to ask.) When your partner asks you a question, listen carefully. Then use the information you read in Step A to answer the questions.

D Listen carefully to the response that Student A gives you. Try to repeat it.

Example:

Oh, I see. So two U.S. holidays are Thanksgiving and Independence Day.

4 Academic Listening and Note Taking

In this section, you will hear and take notes on a two-part lecture given by Nelson Rodgers, a lecturer at a university. The title of his lecture is "The Structure of the U.S. Federal Government." First, Mr. Rodgers will describe the three branches of the U.S. government. Then he will explain the system of checks and balances.

BEFORE THE LECTURE

1 Listening for the plan of a lecture Ⓛ Ⓝ

> Good lecturers usually begin by stating the main topics they plan to talk about, and they often use phrases to signal the order in which they will introduce them. Recognizing this information will give you a good idea of the outline of the lecture and help you organize your notes more effectively.
>
> *What I'm going to do today is . . .*
> *Today, I'm going to discuss . . .*
> *First, I'm going to . . .*
> *First, I plan to . . .*
> *Then I'll talk about . . .*
> *After that . . .*
> *Next, we'll look at . . .*
> *Finally, I'll . . .*

A Form complete sentences from the introduction to Nelson Rodgers's lecture by drawing a line from each item on the left to the correct item on the right.

_____ **1.** First, I'll introduce the three

_____ **2.** And that way, you can start to

_____ **3.** What I'm going to do today is

_____ **4.** And then, after that, I'll explain

_____ **5.** And I'll be using

a. understand how it works.

b. give you an overview of how the government is organized.

c. branches of government.

d. the system of checks and balances.

e. this chart here on the board to help you understand.

B Now put the sentences in Step A in order. Show the order by putting numbers in the spaces provided.

C Watch or listen to the introduction to the lecture and check your answers to Steps A and B.

2 Using information the lecturer puts on the board

Lecturers often write important information on the board, and you should include this information in your notes. As soon as you enter the classroom and sit down, take out your writing materials and copy anything the lecturer has written on the board into your notebook. As the lecture continues, copy anything else the lecturer writes on the board into your notes.

Before the lecture, Mr. Rodgers wrote the chart below on the board. You will use it to take notes when you watch or listen to the first part of the lecture. (Notice that some of the information has already been filled in for you as an example.)

Branch of Government	Legislative	Executive	Judicial
Name	Congress: - Senate - House of Representatives		
Name of officials	senators representatives		
Responsibility	makes laws		
Details	Senate = 100 members (2 from each state) House = 435 members		

1 Guessing vocabulary from context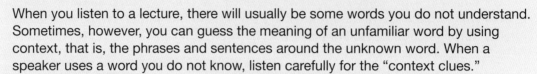

When you listen to a lecture, there will usually be some words you do not understand. Sometimes, however, you can guess the meaning of an unfamiliar word by using context, that is, the phrases and sentences around the unknown word. When a speaker uses a word you do not know, listen carefully for the "context clues."

A The following conversation contains important vocabulary from Part 1 of the lecture. Work with a partner. Using the context and your knowledge of related words, take turns guessing the meanings of the words in **bold**.

Nancy: Did you understand the reading the professor assigned for homework? There were a lot of words I didn't know.

Bill: Really? Well, don't worry too much. It was just an (1) **overview** of the structure of the federal government.

Nancy: Can you explain some things to me? You've (2) **obviously** done the reading.

Bill: Sure. Well, let's see. Did you review the information about the different government (3) **departments**? The heads of those departments are called secretaries, like secretary of state or secretary of defense.

Nancy: Oh, I see. They're part of the executive branch, right?

Bill: That's right. The executive branch also includes the vice president, (4) **besides** the president, of course. And that's the branch that "executes," or (5) **approves**, the laws that Congress makes.

Nancy: You seem to know a lot about this topic!

Bill: Well, I like politics. And I want to do my oral report on (6) **courts** in the United States. I think it's really interesting how they (7) **interpret** the laws that Congress passes.

Nancy: What do you mean?

Bill: Well, the courts decide if a law is (8) **constitutional** or not.

Nancy: Thanks, Bill! I'm going to sit next to you in class today!

B Work with your partner. Match the vocabulary terms from Step A with their definitions. Write the number on the line. Check your answers in a dictionary if necessary.

_____ **a.** clearly, of course

_____ **b.** allows, accepts

_____ **c.** follows, or agrees with, the Constitution of the United States

_____ **d.** in addition to

_____ **e.** parts of the government, or organizations that deal with one specific area

_____ **f.** a general description

_____ **g.** places where judges listen to legal cases

_____ **h.** to decide on the exact meaning of (a law)

2 Using information the lecturer puts on the board

A Watch or listen to Part 1 of the lecture and fill in the missing information in the chart on page 15.

B With your partner, review the information you wrote in your chart. On a separate piece of paper, use the information to write six complete sentences about the lecture content.

Example:

The responsibility of the legislative branch is to make laws.

LECTURE PART 2   The System of Checks and Balances

1 Guessing vocabulary from context ⓥ

A The following items contain important vocabulary from Part 2 of the lecture. Work with a partner. Using the context and your knowledge of related words, take turns guessing the meanings of the words in **bold**.

_____ **1.** The founding fathers . . . wanted to avoid a **dictatorship**.

_____ **2.** Let's **suppose** Congress passes a law, but the president doesn't want to approve it.

_____ **3.** There are times when people **challenge** the constitutionality of a law.

_____ **4.** Most cases like that will be **heard** in a lower-level court.

_____ **5.** The Supreme Court has the final **authority** to decide if the law . . . is either constitutional or unconstitutional.

B Work with your partner. Match the vocabulary terms from Step A with their definitions below. Write the letter on the line. Check your answers in a dictionary if necessary.

a. rule by one party or person

b. power

c. judged

d. imagine

e. question, oppose

2 Taking good lecture notes ⓝ ⓛ ⓢ

Learning to take good notes takes time and practice. Everyone has a unique way of taking notes, but almost everyone follows these guidelines.

- Write only important words, not complete sentences.
- Include main ideas, examples, and important details.
- Indent examples and details.
- Use abbreviations and symbols.

A Look at a student's notes as you watch or listen to Part 2 of the lecture.

The System of Checks and Balances

Why is fed. gov. divided into branches?

    Founders wanted to avoid dictatorship

    Invented system of checks & balances

    3 branches have sep respons. +

    Have power to check (limit) each other's actions

Ex:

    1. Selection of Supreme Court Justices

       - pres. chooses Justices, but Cong. can disapprove

    2. Cong. passes laws, but pres. can veto

    3. Cong. passes law & pres. signs, but Supreme Court can say it's unconstitutional

---

B Work with a partner. Find places where the note taker

- wrote only important words instead of complete sentences;
- wrote main ideas;
- indented examples and details; and
- used abbreviations and symbols.

AFTER THE LECTURE

Sharing your knowledge Ⓢ

Work in small groups. Look at the pictures of the three branches of the U.S. government. Discuss the photos, sharing what you have learned about each branch.

The U.S. Congress
(legislative branch)

The Supreme Court
(judicial branch)

The President
(executive branch)

Chapter 2
Constitutional Issues Today

1 Getting Started

In this section, you are going to read background information about the U.S. Constitution and listen to a time line about some important events in U.S. constitutional history.

1 Reading and thinking about the topic

A Read the following passage.

In 1776, the 13 American colonies declared their independence from Britain. This led to the Revolutionary War, which the British lost in 1783. In 1787, George Washington, James Madison, Alexander Hamilton, and other leaders of the time met in Philadelphia to discuss how to organize the government of the new country, the United States of America. Their work produced the document that set up the structure of government in the United States: the U.S. Constitution. The writers knew that changes to the Constitution would be necessary from time to time as the country grew and changed. Therefore, they created a process for changing, or amending, the original document. Twenty-seven amendments have been added since the Constitution was signed. The first 10 amendments, added in 1791, are called the *Bill of Rights*. Freedom of speech, freedom of religion, and the right to have a lawyer when accused of a crime are three of the basic rights guaranteed by these amendments.

Some parts of the Bill of Rights are controversial today. That is, Americans do not always agree about the correct way to interpret them. According to the Fourth Amendment, for example, government officials, such as police officers, cannot enter people's homes or listen to their phone conversations without permission from a judge. However, some Americans believe the government should be able to do these things if it is looking for information that can help stop terrorism.

Censorship, or limiting freedom of expression in speech, writing, or art, is another example of a controversial issue. For example, some cities and states have tried to pass laws allowing the censorship of works of art or literature that the citizens of those places thought were offensive. Yet these laws conflict with the First Amendment, which gives Americans freedom of speech and freedom of the press.

Whenever there are conflicts like these, it is the responsibility of the courts to decide what is constitutional and what is not.

B Answer the following questions according to the information in the passage.

1. What does the passage say about the history of the U.S. Constitution?

2. What is the Bill of Rights?

3. What are some controversial topics in the U.S. Constitution?

C Read these questions and share your answers with a partner.

1. Do you think it is important for a country to have a written constitution?

2. Do you know of any countries that have a constitution similar to the constitution of the United States?

2 Understanding numbers, dates, and time expressions Ⓝ Ⓛ Ⓢ

Numbers that are used for counting are called *cardinal numbers*. Numbers that are used for describing an order are called o*rdinal numbers*. Numbers can be hard to understand in rapid speech, so it is useful to review their pronunciation.

Cardinal number
"1" is said as *one*.
"2" is said as *two*.
"3" is said as *three*.
"4" is said as *four*.

Ordinal number
first (twenty-first, thirty-first, etc.)
second (twenty-second, thirty-second, etc.)
third (twenty-third, thirty-third, etc.)
fourth (fifth, sixth, seventh, etc.; twenty-fourth, twenty-fifth, etc.)

Dates
"1876" is said as *eighteen seventy-six*.
"2004" is said as *two thousand four*.
"July 4, 1776" is said as *July fourth, seventeen seventy-six*.

Time expressions
in is used with years	*in 1776*
on is used with dates	*on July 4*
during is used with a period of time	*during the 1960s*
between . . . and . . .	*between 1960 and 1990*
from . . . to . . .	*from 1960 to 1990*

A The time line on page 21 shows some important events in U.S. constitutional history. Work in small groups and see if you know or can guess any of the dates. If you think you know a date, fill it in.

🔊 **B** Listen to the time line. Write the dates you hear.

C Work with a partner. Practice repeating the information in the time line. Focus on the correct way of saying numbers, dates, and time expressions.

Example:
On July 4, 1776, the United States declared its independence from Britain.

Important Events in U.S. Constitutional History

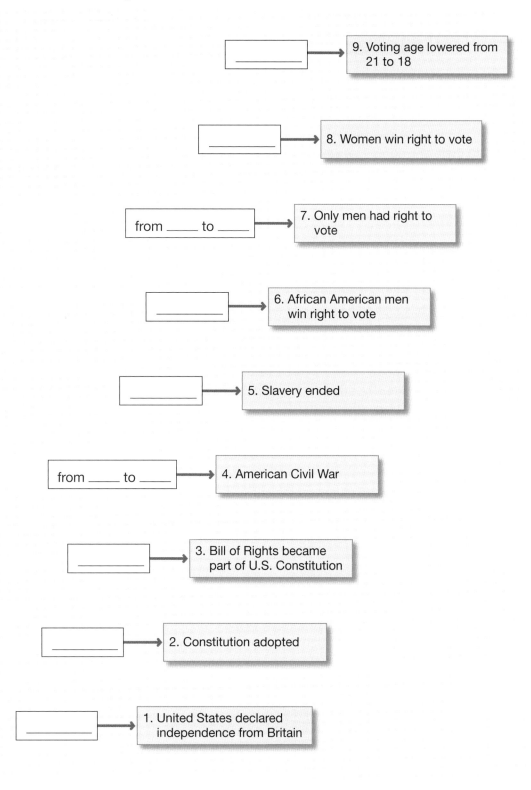

9. Voting age lowered from 21 to 18

8. Women win right to vote

from ____ to ____

7. Only men had right to vote

6. African American men win right to vote

5. Slavery ended

from ____ to ____

4. American Civil War

3. Bill of Rights became part of U.S. Constitution

2. Constitution adopted

1. United States declared independence from Britain

2 Real-Life Voices

In this section, you will hear three people – Magda, Hang, and Gloria – talk about constitutional rights that are important to them.

BEFORE THE INTERVIEWS

1 Sharing your opinion ⓢ

Work with a partner and discuss the following questions.

1. What are some legal rights that you have? Of these rights, which is the most important?
2. Are there any rights that you would like to have, but do not? What are they?
3. Are you aware of any controversies about the rights that people should have? Explain.

2 Previewing the topic ⓢ ⓥ

A Read the following list. It shows some legal rights that Americans have.
If you are American, you can

_____ **a.** send a letter to a newspaper criticizing the president.

_____ **b.** speak to a lawyer if you are arrested by the police.

_____ **c.** buy a gun to use for sport or self-protection.

_____ **d.** refuse to allow the police to enter your home without permission from a judge.

_____ **e.** listen to music (or read books or watch movies) with content that is violent and/or sexual.

_____ **f.** hang a religious symbol outside your house.

_____ **g.** wear any clothes you choose.

_____ **h.** refuse to answer questions that a judge asks you in court.

_____ **i.** look at pictures on the Internet of people in intimate situations.

B Read the information below about some of the amendments in the Bill of Rights. Fill in the blanks in Step A with the number of the amendment that gives Americans each right.

First Amendment	People have freedom of religion, speech, and the press.
Second Amendment	People have the right to "bear arms," that is, to own guns.
Fourth Amendment	People have the right to "be secure in their persons, houses, papers, and effects." This means citizens have the right to privacy and safety in their homes.
Fifth Amendment	In court, people accused of a crime cannot be forced to give evidence against themselves.
Sixth Amendment	People accused of a crime have the right to a speedy (fast) and public trial by jury, and they have the right to be defended by a lawyer.

C Work in small groups and compare your answers. Then discuss the following questions.

1. Do you think the rights listed above are important? Why or why not?

2. Are there countries you know about where people don't have these rights? Explain.

INTERVIEW 1 Important Constitutional Rights

1 Examining vocabulary in context Ⓥ

Here are some words and phrases from the interview with Magda and Hang. Using the context and your knowledge of related words, take turns guessing the meanings of the words in **bold**.

In art, freedom of expression is **critical**: *extremely important*

I believe **censorship** is wrong: *prohibiting or limiting the free expression of words or ideas*

The government has always censored **violent** photographs during wartime: *extremely forceful*

Sometimes works of art or works of literature are **banned** because someone considers them **offensive**: *prohibited/unpleasant, insulting*

I value the fact that in the United States, we have **freedom of assembly**: *the freedom to meet in groups*

This includes the right to **demonstrate** and **complain** and demand change: *express strong opinions about issues in public, especially by marching in the streets in large groups / say you are unhappy or dissatisfied*

The students wanted the university to stop buying products from companies that use **child labor**: *child workers, for example, in factories*

The university changed its **policy**: *rules, official way of doing something*

So you see, our **protests** were very effective: *demonstrations, complaints*

2 Listening for specific information Ⓛ Ⓢ

Sometimes textbooks or teachers provide lists of questions to help you focus on specific information in a listening passage or lecture. If you have access to this information, use it carefully. Read the questions before listening so that you know what information to listen for. If you can, use your background knowledge to try to predict the correct answers. These strategies can help you become a more efficient listener.

A Read the following incomplete sentences and the two possible ways to complete them.

1. The constitutional right that Magda mentions is
   a. the right to attend public protests.
   b. the right to freedom of speech.

2. Magda is a
   a. photographer.
   b. painter.

3. Magda thinks that
   a. artists should be able to paint or draw anything they like.
   b. it's necessary to censor some types of art.

4. Magda says that censorship
   a. happens all the time.
   b. is not very common.

5. Hang says that U.S. citizens have
   a. freedom of assembly.
   b. the right to practice any religion they choose.

6. Hang is a
   a. law student.
   b. medical student.

7. Recently, students at Hang's college
   a. protested the college's policies.
   b. wrote a letter to the college president.

8. Hang is concerned about child labor
   a. in the United States.
   b. in other countries.

B Now listen to the interview. Listen for the answers that correctly complete the sentences and circle them. Then work with a partner and check your answers.

C Discuss these questions in small groups: Do you agree with Magda's and Hang's opinions? Why or why not?

1 Examining vocabulary in context ⓥ

Here are some words and phrases from the interview with Gloria, printed in **bold** and given in the context in which you will hear them. They are followed by definitions.

Can you **identify** an important constitutional right?: *name*

The right to **bear arms** is important to me: *have a gun*

One [group] is **criminals**: *people who act against the law*

Some people have guns for sports, like **hunting** or **target shooting**: *chasing and killing animals for food or sport / shooting a gun at an object for sport*

2 Listening for specific information Ⓛ Ⓢ

A Before you listen to the interview with Gloria, read the paragraph below and predict the kind of information you need to listen for.

Gloria focuses on the right to (1) _____ . She believes the (2) _____ Amendment gives American citizens this right. Gloria says there are (3) _____ groups of people who own guns. One group is (4) _____ , and they will own guns whether it is (5) _____ or not. The second group is (6) _____ people who own guns for (7) _____ reasons, for example, for (8) _____ or for (9) _____ . Gloria explains that the (10) _____ can't be everywhere, so some people might feel that they (11) _____ a gun to protect themselves.

B Listen to the interview. Fill in the blanks in Step A with the missing words or expressions. Then work with a partner and check your responses.

C Discuss Gloria's opinion in small groups. Do you agree or disagree with her? Why?

3 Listening for stressed words Ⓛ Ⓢ

When speakers want to stress an idea, they often stress a particular word in a sentence by saying it louder or more slowly. Look at these examples:

I believe censorship is wrong. (The speaker stresses her own opinion, but other people may disagree with her.)

*I believe censorship is **WRONG**.* (The speaker stresses that censorship is not right.)

Look at the chart and then listen to excerpts from the interview.
Choose your answers after listening to the recording.

Excerpts	Which word does the speaker stress?	What does the speaker mean?
1. The words of the Second Amendment aren't exactly clear.	a. second b. clear	c. The Second Amendment is not as clear as the other amendments. d. The Second Amendment is not really clear. It is a little unclear.
2. Some people have guns for sports.	a. guns b. sports	c. There are different reasons why people have guns. d. Some people have guns, but others have other weapons, like knives.
3. The police can't always protect people.	a. police b. always	c. It is impossible for the police to protect people, but perhaps people can protect themselves. d. The police can protect people sometimes but not all the time.

Understanding humor about the topic ⓢ

> Many jokes and cartoons play with words and their meanings – they use common words and phrases in unexpected ways. Being able to appreciate humor shows that you understand a language on different levels.

A Look at the cartoon and read the caption.

"The way I see it, the Constitution cuts both ways. The First Amendment gives you the right to say what you want, but the Second Amendment gives me the right to shoot you for it."

B Work with a partner or a small group and answer the following questions.

1. Where are the people in the cartoon? What are they doing?
2. What does the speaker mean when he says the Constitution "cuts both ways"?
3. Is the speaker's description of the First and Second Amendments correct?
4. Is the speaker serious? How do you know?
5. Do you think the cartoon is funny? Why or why not?

3 In Your Own Voice

In this section, you will participate in role plays about two controversial situations. Then you will share your opinions about the situations with your classmates.

Role-playing Ⓢ

> Role-playing is a conversation activity in which you pretend that you are a person in an imaginary situation. Role-playing gives you an opportunity to practice new vocabulary and develop your communication skills. This will give you confidence when you need to use the same language and skills in the real world.

A Read the situations below.

Situation 1: A Meeting at School

Pete is a student at a public high school who is very critical of the government's policies. At school, he wears a shirt making a joke about the president. Another student, Nancy, is offended by the joke on the shirt and tells her parents about it. Then Nancy's parents call the school and complain to the principal. The principal invites all four parents to a meeting to discuss the issue. The principal must decide whether to ask Pete to stop wearing the shirt to school.

Roles:
- Pete's parents, who believe Pete has the constitutional right to wear the shirt
- Nancy's parents, who are offended by Pete's shirt
- The principal, who listens to both sides and must make a decision

Situation 2: A Conversation Between Parents

Beatrice, a 10-year-old, often goes to play at the home of Noah, a neighbor. One day Beatrice's parents discover that Noah's parents own a gun. Noah's parents say the gun is locked in a cabinet, but Beatrice's parents are worried about allowing their child to play at the neighbor's house. They decide to talk to Noah's parents because they must decide whether to allow their child to play at Noah's house.

Roles:
- Beatrice's parents, who ask Noah's parents to remove the gun from their home
- Noah's parents, who feel they need the gun for protection

Situation 3: A Conversation Between Parents and Teachers

Ms. Richardson, a middle school teacher, has become very annoyed at the children in her class, who bring their phones to school and use them to text their friends during class time. She and some other teachers told the students that cell phones were banned in school. Some parents are angry at this decision. They say their children need to carry phones so that they can be reached in an emergency.

Roles:
- Ms. Richardson and another teacher, who do not want to allow cell phones in school
- Students' parents, who feel their children need to carry phones

Situation 4: A Problem at the Airport

There is a heated debate at the airport between two passengers and the airport employees. The security guards search the passengers as they go through airport security. The passengers have to remove their belts and stand for a long time. They say that this is an invasion of their privacy.

Roles:
- The two passengers, who think that the searches are unreasonable
- The airport security guards, who say they are just doing their jobs

B Work in small groups. Select one of the situations to role-play. Decide who will play each role. Practice your role play in your group.

C Perform your role play for another group or the class.

D Discuss the situations with members of your class. What would you want if you were the people in these situations?

4 Academic Listening and Note Taking

In this section, you will hear and take notes on a two-part lecture given by Marcella Bencivenni, a professor of U.S. history. The title of her lecture is "The First Amendment." Professor Bencivenni will give an overview of the First Amendment to the Constitution and discuss some controversies that surround it.

BEFORE THE LECTURE

1 Predicting what you will hear ⓢ

> Thinking about the topic and trying to predict what you will hear will greatly increase your understanding.

A Read the following excerpts from introductions to newspaper articles based on true stories.

1.

Protest for Immigrant Rights

Last Friday, the streets of Los Angeles were filled with hundreds of thousands of people protesting the government's policies on immigration.

2.

Newspaper Publishes Controversial Cartoon

Although a recent cartoon was likely to offend some religious groups, a newspaper made the decision to publish it.

3.

Controversy over Soldier's Record

A soldier said he received a medal for bravery in the army, but other officers claimed that this was not true. The court must now decide on whether to convict him or not.

4.

Police Officer Fired for Wearing Religious Symbol on Uniform

After receiving two warnings, a Texas police officer was fired for wearing a small religious symbol on the collar of his police uniform.

5.

Library Takes Book off Shelves

To Kill a Mockingbird, Harper Lee's classic American novel about discrimination and personal choice, has too much sex and disturbing racial themes, according to some readers.

6.

Controversial Speaker Invited to College Campus

Despite student protests, a speaker was invited to make a presentation at a New York college graduation. The speaker used humor to make fun of the government.

B With a partner, discuss the following questions.

1. In each article, what rights are exercised by the people involved?
2. Do you think any of these topics is controversial? Why or why not?
3. Based on these excerpts, what topics do you think the lecturer will discuss?

2 Listening for main ideas and details Ⓛ Ⓝ Ⓢ

Remember that *main ideas* are the important points a speaker wants to make. *Supporting details* explain, describe, or prove main ideas. Supporting details may include definitions, examples, reasons, explanations, or stories, or simply provide additional information. For example:

Main idea
I'm going to talk about a very important right: freedom of speech.

Supporting detail (additional information)
Freedom of speech is protected by the Bill of Rights.

A Below are two excerpts from the lecture. The sentences are not in the correct order. Read the sentences and write the number *1* next to the main idea. Then predict the order of the other sentences by writing the numbers *2–6* in the blanks.

Excerpt 1

- _____ For instance, an employer can't hire you or fire you just because he likes or doesn't like your religion.
- _____ Freedom of religion is a very important right.
- _____ What I mean is, Americans are free to wear any kind of religious clothing they prefer.
- _____ Now this freedom affects Americans in many ways.
- _____ Basically it means two things: First, Americans are free to practice their religion without interference from the government, and second, there is no national religion.
- _____ And freedom of religion even includes how you dress.

Excerpt 2

- _____ In fact, the courts have said that freedom of speech includes all forms of expression, meaning words, pictures, music . . . even the way you wear your hair!
- _____ You're also free to read or listen to other people's ideas.
- _____ The next freedom listed in the First Amendment is maybe the most famous one, because it's the one that all of us practice every single day, and that's freedom of speech.
- _____ But in addition, freedom of speech includes what we call "symbolic" speech – like wearing the clothes you like.
- _____ Basically, it means you're free to talk openly about your ideas even if other people disagree with them.
- _____ What does that mean, exactly?

B Watch or listen to the two excerpts. Check to see if you correctly selected the main idea and if you placed the other sentences in the correct order.

LECTURE PART 1 Overview of the First Amendment

1 Guessing vocabulary from context

A The following book review contains important vocabulary from Part 1 of the lecture. Work with a partner. Using context clues, take turns guessing the meanings of the words in **bold**.

A new book, *Looking Again at the First Amendment*, analyzes recent (1) **cases** that show why the right to freedom of speech is so controversial. The book begins with an overview of the history behind the First Amendment, which of course, (2) **guarantees** the five freedoms many of us take for granted. Then it goes on to show how the amendment (3) **affects** the way we live every day.

What makes this new book so interesting are the different examples it includes. Freedom of religion is a complex issue these days. Airport security procedures now require people to remove belts, jackets, and hats, but what about turbans? American Sikhs say that they should be allowed to practice their religion without (4) **interference** from the government. After all, they point out, an employer can't (5) **hire** or fire you because of your religion, and security guards shouldn't be able to make it difficult to travel because of your religion, either.

Under U.S. law, (6) **journalists** can write articles that (7) **criticize** the government, but does this freedom of (8) **expression** have limits? The book describes how newspaper articles about (9) **military** involvement in war typically include very few photographs. This is controversial, too, because some people think that this limits the power of the (10) **press** and hides the extent of U.S. participation in these wars.

All in all, the book does an excellent job at showing how complex the First Amendment is.

B Work with your partner. Match the vocabulary terms from Step A with their definitions below. Write the number on the line. Check your answers in a dictionary if necessary.

_____ **a.** magazine and newspaper writers

_____ **b.** influences, has an effect on

_____ **c.** unwanted involvement or participation

_____ **d.** give someone a job

_____ **e.** say negative things about someone or something

_____ **f.** promises

_____ **g.** relating to soldiers or war

_____ **h.** written materials that bring people news; also, the people who write these materials

_____ **i.** situations, examples

_____ **j.** communication of thoughts or feelings

2 Using symbols and abbreviations Ⓝ Ⓛ Ⓢ

When you are taking notes during a lecture, you have to write down a lot of information very quickly. To save time, use symbols and abbreviations whenever you can. Some forms are commonly used. Here are some examples:

Common symbols

+ OR &	and		. . .	and so on / etc.
%	percent		→	leads to / causes
∴	therefore		"	ditto (same as above)
=	equals / is / has		↑, ↓	increase / decrease
≠	not / not the same as		> / <	more than / less than

Common abbreviations

e.g. OR ex	for example		w/	with
b/c	because		w/o	without
esp.	especially		etc.	and so on
imp.	important		i.e.,	that is (in other words)
vs	versus (against)		yr.	year
pt	part		inc.	include / including
sum	summary / summarize			

A Study the following list of important words and suggested abbreviations from Part 1 of the lecture.

Word	Abbreviation	Word	Abbreviation	Word	Abbreviation
amendment	*amend*	freedom	*f'dom*	religion	*relig*
different	*diff*	students	*sts*	president	*pres*
government	*gov't*	Americans	*Ams*	expression	*exp*
speech	*spch*	representatives	*reps*	group	*grp*
includes / including	*inc.*	without	*w/o*	articles	*arts.*

B Read the incomplete notes on page 34. Work in pairs and predict which symbols or abbreviations from the box and Step A will go in the blanks.

C Watch or listen to Part 1 of the lecture. Complete the notes, using symbols and abbreviations from the box and Step A.

D Work with a partner and compare your answers. Summarize the First Amendment in your own words.

1st _____ 5 f'doms
1. F'dom of _____
   = _____ can practice their _____ _____
   interference from _____
   U.S. has no national _____
2. F'dom of _____
   = _____ to talk openly about ideas
   _____ "symbolic speech" like clothes
   _____ all forms of _____ , meaning words, pictures
3. _____ of the press
   = _____ to publish _____ ideas & opinions
   inc. books, newspapers, magazine + Internet _____
   cartoon making joke about _____ is legal
   journalist can write article criticizing the _____
4. _____ of assembly
   = can meet in _____
   _____ can participate in college demonstration
5. _____ of petition
   = citizens have _____ to ask _____ to change things
   To sum: we use the term _____ of _____ to talk about
   all 5 _____ .

LECTURE PART 2 First Amendment Controversies

1 Guessing vocabulary from context Ⓥ

A The following items contain important vocabulary from Part 2 of the lecture. Work with a partner. Using the context and your knowledge of related words, take turns guessing the meanings of the words in **bold**.

_____ **1. In practice**, there are some restrictions [on freedom of speech].

_____ **2.** They think flag burning is **unpatriotic** and insults the country.

_____ **3.** The Supreme Court has **ruled** that flag burning is legal.

_____ **4.** Many teachers and principals . . . have tried to **forbid** cell phones [at school].

_____ **5.** Parents say they need to have a way to **get in touch with** their children.

_____ **6.** Do you think children should have the right to say prayers in **public schools**?

B Work with your partner. Match the vocabulary terms in Step A with their definitions below. Write the letters in the blanks next to the sentence containing the correct term in Step A. Check your answers in a dictionary if necessary.

a. not allow

b. contact (for example, by phone)

c. in reality; the way people actually do something

d. showing lack of love or respect for your country

e. decided (a legal case)

f. free schools that are paid for by taxes

2 Using a map to organize your notes Ⓝ Ⓛ Ⓢ

Some people like to take notes using a method called *mapping*. One way to make a map is to write the topic or the main idea in the center of the page. The supporting details are written under, over, or next to the main idea. Related ideas are connected by lines.

A Below is a section of a student's map for Part 2 of the lecture. Study the map with a partner and answer these questions: What is this part of the lecture about? How many examples are given? What information is missing?

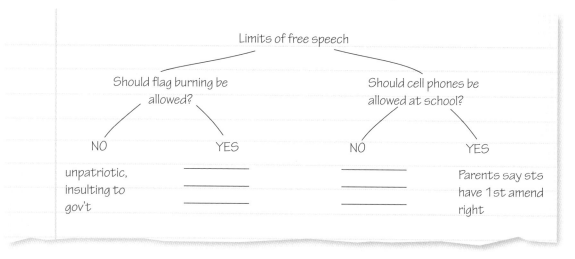

Limits of free speech

Should flag burning be allowed?

Should cell phones be allowed at school?

NO — unpatriotic, insulting to gov't

YES

NO

YES — Parents say sts have 1st amend right

B Now look at another section of the map. Answer these questions with your partner: What is the main idea? What is the example? Where do you predict you will need to draw lines to connect ideas?

What does f'dom of relig mean in practice?

e.g. Allow children to pray in pub. schools?

YES
1st amend guar. f'dom of relig.

NO
1st amend also says no nat'l relig. Schools = public, so no relig. activity allowed

Courts say: Private prayer OK, but if org'd by school – no

🔊 **C** Now watch or listen to Part 2 of the lecture. Fill in the missing information in Step A. Draw in the missing lines in Step B.

D Work in small groups and compare answers. Then use the maps to answer these questions.

1. What are the limits of free speech?
2. What does freedom of religion mean in practice?

Conducting a survey Ⓝ Ⓢ

> The purpose of a survey is to collect information in order to compare the opinions of different individuals or groups of people. Surveys usually consist of questions for interviewees to answer or statements that interviewees are asked to agree or disagree with. Interviewers often ask follow-up questions to allow the interviewees to give more information or explain their opinions.

A You are going to survey three people outside your class about four controversial questions.

1. Do you think it should be legal to burn the flag as a form of political protest?
2. Do you think children should be allowed to bring cell phones to school?
3. Do you think teachers and students in public schools should have the right to say a prayer together at the beginning of the school day?
4. Do you think the government should be allowed to listen to people's telephone conversations?

B On your own paper, make four charts like the one below, one for each question.

Question:				
Person	**Opinion**			**Reason**
	Yes	Not sure	No	
	Yes	Not sure	No	
	Yes	Not sure	No	

C Try to talk to people of different ages and backgrounds. Here is a way to start:
Hi. I'm doing a survey for my English class about controversial issues.
May I ask you a few questions? Please answer yes, no, *or* I'm not sure.

D After a person has answered a question, follow up by asking *Why?*
Take notes on the person's reason(s) in your chart.

E Explain the results of your survey to a small group or to the class.
Give your own opinion about the questions as well.

Unit 1 Academic Vocabulary Review

This section reviews the vocabulary from Chapters 1 and 2. Some of the words you needed to learn to understand the content of this unit are specific to its topics. Other words are more general. They appear across different academic fields and are extremely useful for all students to know. For a complete list of all the Academic Word List words in this book, see the Appendix on page 182.

A Read the news articles. The boxes include pairs of related words. Choose the correct word from each pair to complete the sentences. You will not use all of the words.

Worried About Nature?

A large public (1) _____ recently showed that (2) _____ pollution is a worry to many people, but finding solutions that work is a big (3) _____ . Recently, the government (4) _____ a new study to research ways that companies could reduce pollution. The study was (5) _____ , but it suggested that companies must take more responsibility for protecting the environment. However, companies said that the proposed solutions were too expensive and criticized the press for overreacting.

authority, authorized
challenge, challenging
conclusion, inconclusive
demonstration, demonstrate
environment, environmental

Are the Police Doing Their Job?

The issue of privacy has become increasingly (6) _____ in recent years. In the Constitution, the (7) _____ fathers laid the basis for the right to privacy. However, this right is difficult to (8) _____ correctly. Some people think the police should be able to ask for a person's (9) _____ if that person is acting in a suspicious way. Others, however, say that is probably unconstitutional and (10) _____ .

controversy, controversial
foundation, founding
identification, unidentified
interpretation, interpret
legality, illegal

Banned from Sports?

For many Muslim women, the headscarf (11) _____ their religious beliefs. One woman, Shariqua Jones, said that for her and her family, wearing the scarf was not a (12) _____ but a matter of personal choice. However, when her daughter wanted to (13) _____ in a sports event, she was asked to remove her scarf. Ms. Jones said that this was not fair. She remarked: "(14) _____ , school officials are not taking this issue seriously enough. Everyone should be treated (15) _____ . My daughter has the same rights as other children."

obvious, obviously
participation, participate
requirement, required
similarity, similarly
symbol, symbolizes

B Use the academic vocabulary from A above to answer the following questions in pairs or as a class.

Voting

1. What are some of the factors that influence people's decision to vote or not vote?
2. How has voter turnout changed over the years?
3. What issues do many people think are important?

The U.S. Government

4. What is the basic structure of the U.S. government?
5. Why is it organized this way?
6. Which officials work for each branch?

The Constitution

7. What is the Constitution?
8. What is the Bill of Rights?
9. What have you learned about the different amendments?

The First Amendment

10. What does the First Amendment include?
11. Why is the First Amendment often controversial?
12. What kinds of things do people disagree about?

Oral Presentation

In academic courses, you will sometimes give oral presentations to a small group about a topic you have researched. Below are some guidelines to keep in mind. Your task is to make a five-minute presentation to a small group of four to five people on an American president of your choice.

BEFORE THE PRESENTATION

1 Research the topic

Choose a president to research (some famous presidents are listed below, but you may choose any). Consult several books or Web sites to find out as much information as you can about them.

Dwight David Eisenhower

Andrew Jackson

Thomas Jefferson

John Fitzgerald Kennedy

James Madison

Abraham Lincoln

Woodrow Wilson

Franklin Delano Roosevelt

Theodore "Teddy" Roosevelt

George Washington

Barack Obama

2 Organize your presentation

Organize your presentation so that you can present the information in an interesting way. You should aim to cover at least the following categories:

Name: _____
Give the president's full name.

Date of presidency: _____
Give the beginning and ending years of the presidency.

Historical context: _____
Explain what was happening in the U.S. at the time this person was president.

Special achievements: _____
Discuss any special achievements of this president.

Interesting facts: _____
Include details that will keep your audience focused on what you are saying.

Your reason for choosing this president: _____

3 Make a handout

Make a one-page handout for your group that includes an outline of your presentation. List the important categories and any visual information you wish to share, but leave space for your classmates to take notes on what you are saying.

DURING THE PRESENTATION

1 Introduce your presentation

It is very important to tell your audience what you are going to speak about and give them some sense of the different ideas you will include.

2 Speak slowly

Remember that you are going to share a lot of information about an unfamiliar topic. Take your time and pronounce each word carefully. From time to time, ask your audience if they have any questions about what you are saying.

3 Refer to the handout

Follow the outline you have prepared and ask your group to take notes on what you are saying.

AFTER THE PRESENTATION

1 Check for comprehension

When you have finished speaking, ask your classmates if they have any questions about what you have said. Make sure they have no questions about your presentation.

2 Thank your audience!

Unit 2
A Diverse Nation

In this unit, you will learn how American society is made up of people from many cultural and ethnic groups. Chapter 3 concerns the wave of immigration to the United States from the mid-nineteenth to the early twentieth century. You will hear interviews with Americans whose families left Europe during that time to begin new lives in this country. The lecture is about the experience of these immigrants. In Chapter 4, you will hear the voices of Americans who arrived in the next wave of immigration, which began during the second half of the twentieth century and continues today. The lecture discusses how these new immigrants have become part of American society while staying connected to their countries and cultures of origin.

Contents

In Unit 2, you will listen to and speak about the following topics.

Skills

In Unit 2, you will practice the following skills.

 Listening Skills

Listening for numerical information
Listening for tone of voice
Listening for specific information
Listening for transitional phrases that introduce supporting details
Listening for percentages and fractions
Listening for stressed words
Listening for definitions

 Speaking Skills

Examining graphics
Answering true/false questions
Retelling what you have heard
Applying what you have learned
Conducting research
Using telegraphic language
Answering multiple-choice questions
Personalizing the topic
Sharing your opinion
Discussing your experience
Previewing the topic

 Vocabulary Skills

Reading and thinking about the topic
Building background knowledge on the topic
Examining vocabulary in context
Guessing vocabulary from context

 Note Taking Skills

Taking notes on handouts
Organizing your notes in columns
Reviewing and revising notes
Using bullets to organize your notes

Learning Outcomes

Prepare and **deliver** an oral presentation in pairs on an interview conducted outside of class

Chapter 3
The Origins of Diversity

Lewis W. Hines was a photographer. He took pictures of immigrants during the early part of the twentieth century. Look at the photo and answer the questions with a partner.

1. What does the photo show? Describe what you see.
2. What does the photo tell you about the family – their background, thoughts, and feelings?

1 Getting Started

In this section, you are going to read some background information about late nineteenth- and early twentieth-century immigration to the United States. You will also hear numerical information and examine graphs about this wave of immigration.

1 Reading and thinking about the topic ⓥ ⓢ

A Read the following passage.

The United States is a country of immigrants. Its people come from a variety of religious, economic, racial, and ethnic backgrounds.

In the early seventeenth century, English settlers began immigrating to America in search of religious freedom. For the next two hundred years, these settlers brought hundreds of thousands of people from Africa to work as slaves. As they continued to establish communities throughout the continent, settlers also encountered different tribes of Native Americans. Many Native Americans died either from diseases brought by the settlers or because of conflict over land.

From the 1840s to the 1920s, another big wave of immigration occurred. This wave of immigrants included Germans, Irish, Italians, and Jews. Smaller groups of Chinese and Mexican immigrants also came to America. Some came in search of better economic opportunities, while others came for political or religious freedom. Some groups were welcomed, and others were rejected. However, they all left their mark on America's economy, society, and culture.

B Answer the following questions according to the information in the passage.

   1. Why is the United States considered a country of immigrants?

   2. What were some of the largest groups of immigrants to come to the United States between the 1840s and the 1920s? Why did they come?

C Read these questions and share your answers with a partner.

   1. Do you know of anyone who immigrated to America in the late nineteenth or early twentieth centuries? Why did they come? What were their experiences?

   2. What do you think would be the most difficult thing about leaving your country and going somewhere else to live?

2 Building background knowledge on the topic

A Read the information on the time line.

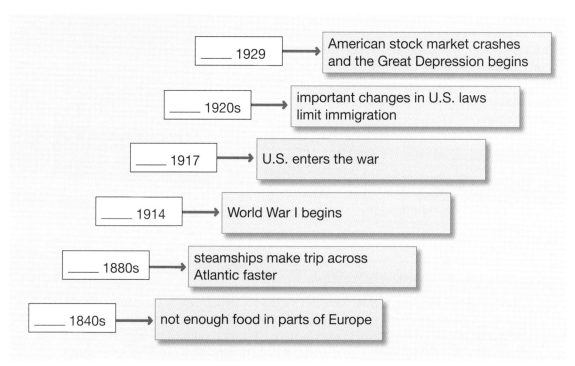

B Work with a partner. Practice making sentences about immigration based on the information in the time line. Make sure to put your sentences in the past tense.

Example:
In the 1840s, there wasn't enough food in some parts of Europe.

C Do you think these factors led to an increase or a decrease in immigration? Write +
(increase) or − (decrease) in the blank next to each event on the time line. Then explain
your ideas to the class.

3 Listening for numerical information

Listening for numbers and dates can be very difficult in a second language. Here are some suggestions to help you understand numerical information about history.

1. Learn the words and phrases often used to refer to time periods.

century = 100 years
twentieth century = 1900–1999
the mid-1930s = around 1935

decade = 10 years
figure = number
the early 1940s = 1940–1943

2. Learn verbs that often describe numbers.
go up = increase, rise, climb
go down = decrease, fall, decline

A Work with a partner and look at the graph below. It shows legal immigration to the United States from 1820 to 2010 according to the U.S. Census Bureau.

B Listen to a description of immigration patterns to the United States. Fill in the missing parts of the graph with the information you hear.

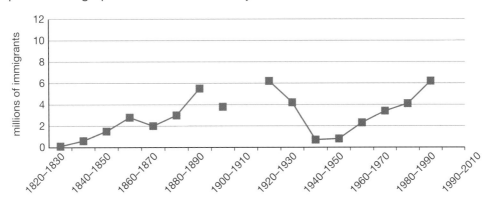

Source: U.S. Census Bureau: Statistical Yearbook Bureau of Citizenship and Immigration Services

C Work with a partner and compare answers. Then discuss this question: What is the main difference between immigration patterns to the United States in the nineteenth and the twentieth centuries?

2 Real-Life Voices

In this section, you will hear three Americans of different ethnic and cultural backgrounds discuss the experiences of their families, who settled in the United States in the late nineteenth and early twentieth centuries.

BEFORE THE INTERVIEWS

1 Building background knowledge on the topic Ⓥ Ⓢ

A Read these two sets of factors that influence immigration. Match each factor with the correct explanation. The first one has been done for you.

"Push" factors: reasons people leave their home countries

_4_ **a.** economic   **1.** There is no freedom to belong to certain political parties.

____ **b.** political   **2.** People must follow the state religion.

____ **c.** religious   **3.** People want to have more adventure.

____ **d.** other   **4.** There are no jobs.

"Pull" factors: reasons people want to come to the United States

____ **a.** economic   **1.** People can express their views about the government.

____ **b.** political   **2.** The country is very beautiful.

____ **c.** religious   **3.** There are more jobs in the United States.

____ **d.** other   **4.** There is freedom to follow your own beliefs.

B Work with a partner and read the statements below. Match each statement with one of the factors in Step A by writing the correct letter in the appropriate column.

Push	Pull	
		1. My great-grandparents came from Italy around 1890. There were more jobs in the United States.
		2. Many people in my grandparents' village in Russia were attacked because of their religious beliefs.
		3. My mother came over to the States to meet up with my father. They were in love and planned to get married.
		4. My parents came from a farming village in Greece because there wasn't enough land there for people to farm.
		5. In 1848, there was a potato famine in Ireland. All the potato plants died, and there was very little food for years after that.
		6. The United States is a democracy. We came to the United States because we wanted to vote for the party of our choice.
		7. In the village we came from, it was dangerous to express your real opinions.

2 Examining graphics ⓢ

A Look at the two pie charts. They show where immigrants to the United States came from during two important periods: from 1840 to 1860 and from 1880 to 1900.

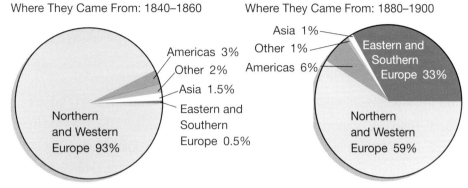

Source: **Historical Statistics of the United States**

B Underline or circle the choice that correctly completes each statement. Then work with a partner and compare your answers.

1. From 1840 to 1860, most immigrants came from (*northern and western Europe / the Americas / Asia / eastern and southern Europe / other places*).

2. Most immigrants from eastern and southern Europe came to the United States in the period (*1840–1860 / 1880–1900*).

3. From 1840 to 1900, the percentage of immigrants from the Americas (*rose a little / stayed exactly the same / fell quickly*).

4. The percentage of immigrants from Asia (*increased a lot / stayed about the same / fell sharply*) during the 1840–1900 time period.

INTERVIEW 1   Immigration to the United States in the 1860s

1 Examining vocabulary in context ⓥ

Here are some words and phrases from the interview with Patrick printed in **bold** and given in the context in which you will hear them. They are followed by definitions.

You see, over in Ireland, people were **desperate**: *without hope*

That was the time when, as you probably know, there was a potato **famine**: *a situation in which people die from hunger because there is not enough food*

It's difficult to **imagine** this, but about a million people died at that time: *believe*

So the Irish started coming over in **massive** numbers: *very large*

They stuck together: *They helped each other.*

They depended on each other to **survive**: *live*

They were Catholic. That set **them apart**: *made them different from other people*

I've heard there was a lot of **prejudice** against them: *negative feelings or opinions*

On the other hand, they **made a lot of contributions to society**: *worked hard to help their families and society*

2 Answering true/false questions Ⓢ Ⓛ

True/false questions might seem easy, but sometimes they are harder than they look. Be sure to read them carefully before answering. Remember these guidelines.

- If part of the statement is false, then the entire statement is false.
- Absolute statements (statements that use words like *all*, *always*, *never*, *nobody*) are usually false.

A Read the statements below before you listen to the interview with Patrick.

_____ **1.** Patrick's grandparents met in the United States.

_____ **2.** Patrick's family came to the United States for political reasons.

_____ **3.** Some of Patrick's relatives stayed in Ireland after his grandparents immigrated to the United States.

_____ **4.** The potato famine happened before Patrick's grandparents left Ireland.

_____ **5.** Many immigrants arrived with less than $50.

_____ **6.** Most Irish immigrants were Catholic.

_____ **7.** Irish immigrants all worked as farmers.

_____ **8.** Patrick comes from a small family.

🔊 **B** Now listen to the interview. Mark each sentence *T* (true) or *F* (false). After listening, work with a partner. Compare answers and correct the false statements.

3 Listening for tone of voice Ⓛ

🔊 Listen again to excerpts from the interview. Circle the response that best describes Patrick's feelings.

Excerpt One

Patrick is explaining how his grandparents immigrated to America.
His grandparents probably felt

a. worried about their new home.

b. concerned about leaving their family behind.

c. excited about their new experience.

Excerpt Two

Patrick is talking about immigration in the mid- to late nineteenth century.
When he explains the historical events of that time, he sounds

a. sad about events in Ireland.

b. confused about his family.

c. interested in the reasons for immigration.

Excerpt Three

Patrick is explaining the contributions that the Irish made to society. He sounds

    a. proud of the role the Irish played in America.

    b. angry about the difficulties the Irish faced.

    c. unsure about the opportunities in America.

INTERVIEW 2   Immigration to the United States in the 1900s

1 Examining vocabulary in context Ⓥ

Here are some words and phrases from the interview with Eunice and John printed in **bold** and given in the context in which you will hear them. They are followed by definitions.

    There was always a fear of **religious persecution**: *being attacked because of your religious beliefs*

    . . . you'd **end up in jail**: *be sent to prison*

    . . . the economy was bad, and they couldn't **make a living**: *earn enough money to live*

    The trip alone was a **nightmare**: *a very difficult experience*

    When they finally arrived, **they were almost penniless**: *they had very little money*

    My father was a good student, and he ended up getting a **scholarship** to college: *a grant or gift of money to pay for college expenses*

    As I **look back on it**, I see that . . . : *remember; think about something in the past*

    . . . my family **struggled** hard: *had to overcome many difficulties*

2 Listening for specific information Ⓛ Ⓝ Ⓢ

A Look at the chart below before you listen to the interview with Eunice and John.

	Eunice	John
Ethnic or religious background	Jewish	
Country their relatives came from		
Reasons their relatives came to the United States		
Experience of their relatives in America		

B Now listen to the interview. Take notes in the chart based on what the speakers say. Then work with a partner and compare answers.

AFTER THE INTERVIEWS

1 Retelling what you have heard Ⓢ

A Review the interviews with Patrick, Eunice, and John. On the lines below, write one question for each speaker. You will use these questions in Step C.

Question for Patrick: _____

Question for Eunice: _____

Question for John: _____

B Form groups of three. Each member of the group will pretend to be Patrick, Eunice, or John. When it is your turn to speak, explain

- when and why your family immigrated to America; and
- what happened to your family after arriving in America.

C Listen as your classmates ask you their questions. Answer the questions the way Patrick, Eunice, and John would answer them.

2 Applying what you have learned ⓢ

Finding ways to apply what you have learned is a good way to deepen your understanding of a topic.

A Read these excerpts from poems about the immigrant experience.

The Famine Year
Jane Francesca Elgee (Lady Wilde) 1826–1896

> Little children, tears are strange upon your infant faces,
> God meant you but to smile within your mother's soft embraces.
> Oh! we know not what is smiling, and we know not what is dying;
> We're hungry, very hungry, and we cannot stop our crying.

Tales of a Hurried Man
Emanuel Carnevali 1897–1942

> O Italy, O great boot,
> Please don't kick me out again.

The New Colossus
Emma Lazarus 1849–1887

> Give me your tired, your poor,
> Your huddled masses yearning to breathe free,
> The wretched refuse of your teeming shore.
> Send these, the homeless, tempest-tossed to me,
> I lift my lamp beside the golden door!

B Work with a partner and discuss what the poets are saying.

Example:
The poet is writing about the effect of famine on children.

C Share your ideas with the class. How is the poem related to the stories you heard in the interviews?

3 In Your Own Voice

In this section, you will learn more about the experiences of the millions of immigrants who came to America during the late nineteenth and early twentieth centuries. First, you will do some research about immigration during this period. Then you will act the role of an immigrant and tell that person's story.

1 Conducting research ⓢ

In academic classes, you will often be asked to do assignments or projects that involve research. You can use a library or the Internet to find information. When you find something useful, make sure you copy it accurately. Always write down the source of the information (the book, magazine, newspaper, or Web site where you found the information).

A You are going to do research on Ellis Island, which is in New York City's harbor. Ellis Island was once the port of entry for millions of immigrants to the United States. Today it is a museum dedicated to telling the story of these immigrants.

B Work in four groups. Each group will be responsible for answering one of the following questions.

    1. When did immigrants come through Ellis Island?

    2. Which immigrant groups came through Ellis Island?

    3. When and why did they come?

    4. What happened to them when they arrived in the United States?

C Go to the Ellis Island Web site at www.ellisisland.org and click on "Ellis Island History" (under "Ellis Island"). If you do not have Internet access, read about Ellis Island in a library. Ask the librarian for help if necessary. Read and take notes on the answer to your assigned question.

D In class, form new groups of four people who each researched a different question. Share the information you found with the other members of your group.

The main building at Ellis Island, about 1900

Today the main building is an immigration museum

2 Applying what you have learned Ⓢ

A The chart below describes immigrants who came to America in the late nineteenth and early twentieth centuries. Select one of the immigrants. Write an imaginary story about his or her immigration experience based on the information you see. You can use these questions as a guide in making up your story:

- Was there one specific event that made you decide to leave your country?
- Was it difficult for you to leave?
- What are your hopes and dreams about your new life in America?
- What worries do you have about the future?

	Martin O'Reilly	**Salvatore Leo**	**Katya Prinz**	**Maria Karas**
Origin	Ireland	Italy	Poland	Greece
Age	25	17	60	10
Occupation	carpenter, wants to start his own business	unemployed but looking for a job in construction	seamstress with a lot of experience	elementary school student
Family status	married	single	widow	single
Religion	Catholic	Catholic	Jewish	Greek Orthodox
Reason for coming	to escape the potato famine and start a new life	to avoid the army and go to college	to gain religious freedom; and to join her son, who came three years earlier	to join her relatives from the same small village, where there were no jobs

Notes:

B Work in groups. Tell your story to your classmates and listen to their stories.

4 Academic Listening and Note Taking

In this section, you will hear and take notes on a two-part lecture given by Gerald Meyer, a professor of U.S. history. The title of his lecture is "Immigrants to America: Challenges and Contributions." Professor Meyer will describe some of the experiences of late nineteenth- and early twentieth-century immigrants to the United States.

BEFORE THE LECTURE

1 Taking notes on handouts Ⓝ

A Below, on the left, is a handout showing a list of readings for Professor Meyer's history class on early immigration to the United States. Fill in the blanks with the missing unit titles and readings from the list on the right.

<table>
<tr><td>

**Early Immigration
to the United States**

Prof. G. Meyer

Assigned Readings

UNIT 1: _____

Readings:

1 <u>Strong Anti-Irish Sentiment Begins to Grow</u>

2 _____

3 _____

UNIT 2: _____

Readings:

1 <u>Many Unskilled Workers Needed for Nation's Infrastructure</u>

2 _____

3 _____

</td><td>

Unit Titles
- Contributions of Immigrant Groups
- Prejudice Toward Immigrant Groups

Readings
- Strong Anti-Irish Sentiment Begins to Grow
- Many Unskilled Workers Needed for Nation's Infrastructure
- Jobs in Construction and Services
- Needs of Agricultural and Industrial Production
- Widespread Anti-Immigrant Feelings
- Religious Prejudice and Stereotypes

</td></tr>
</table>

B Work with a partner and compare answers.
Use the information in the handout to predict what you will hear in the lecture.

2 Listening for transitional phrases that introduce supporting details ⓛ Ⓝ Ⓢ

Supporting details consist of specific information such as reasons, explanations, examples, facts, and definitions. Lecturers often introduce supporting details with transitional phrases like the following.

Type of supporting detail	Transitional phrase
Reason	*a/the/one reason for this is/was that . . .*
	a/the/one reason for this is/was because . . .
Explanation	*what I mean is . . . , in other words, . . .*
Example	*for instance, . . . for example, . . .*
	like/such as . . .
Fact	*in fact, . . . / actually, . . .*
Definition	*by X, I mean . . . / X means . . .*

A Read the following excerpts from the lecture. Predict which transitions from the box above the lecturer will use.

1. The four major groups that immigrated to the U.S. during this time were Germans, Irish, Jews from eastern Europe, and Italians. Of course, there were many other immigrants – _____ , from Greece, Hungary, China, and Mexico.

2. Some Americans were worried about the size and diversity of the new foreign population. You have to remember that millions of immigrants arrived during this time, _____ , almost 30 million of them.

3. Most people in the United States were Protestants, and they were often prejudiced against the Catholics and also against the Jews. _____ the immigrants' religious practices and traditions seemed strange to them.

4. The Irish, on the other hand, helped build the infrastructure of many American cities – _____ , the canals, the bridges, the railroads, the seaports, and the roads.

B Now watch or listen to the excerpts and fill in the blanks with the transitions you hear.

1 Guessing vocabulary from context Ⓥ

A The following conversation contains important vocabulary from Part 1 of the lecture. Work with a partner. Using the context and your knowledge of related words, take turns guessing the meanings of the words in **bold**.

Nadine: I was reviewing the chapter on early immigration to the U.S. I can't believe some of the difficulties those immigrants faced.

Raul: Yeah, right? First of all, let's see, the chapter says: "they (1) **crowded** into big cities." That must have been a very (2) **frightening** experience. Can you imagine coming from a tiny village to New York or Chicago?

Nadine: Yes, and that wasn't the only problem they faced. I also read that some immigrants were seen as a (3) **threat** to the American way of life.

Raul: What, were they seen as being (4) **unpatriotic** or something?

Nadine: Sure, because many of them didn't speak English and plus, some Americans were afraid that the immigrants wouldn't share their (5) **democratic values**.

Raul: It's sad in a way. Why are people so (6) **cruel** to each other?

Nadine: I don't know. I guess it's just hard for some people to accept newcomers.

B Work with your partner. Match the vocabulary terms from Step A with their definitions below. Write the words on the line. Check your answers in a dictionary if necessary.

a. hurtful, unfair _____

b. beliefs in democracy _____

c. large numbers moved into small spaces _____

d. danger _____

e. making people afraid or scared _____

f. not loyal to their country _____

2 Using telegraphic language Ⓛ Ⓢ Ⓝ

Telegraphic language consists mainly of words that convey information – nouns, verbs, adjectives, and adverbs. It usually does not include articles (*a*, *an*, and *the* or the verb *be*). You have probably seen telegraphic language in newspaper headlines. When you take notes, you should use telegraphic language, abbreviations, and symbols to save time. For example:

You hear: *The four major groups that immigrated to the U.S. during this time were Germans, Irish, Jews from eastern Europe, and Italians.*

You write: *4 maj grps imm'ed to U.S.: Germans, Irish, Jews (eastern Europe), Italians*

A Look at the incomplete outline of Part 1 of Professor Meyer's lecture on the next page. Predict the kind of information you need to complete the notes.

<u>Imm's Face Prejudice</u>

I. _____

Germans, Irish, Jews (eastern Europe), Italians

II. Prejudice

Ex: _____ , refuse to rent them apt. or give them jobs

III. _____

A. _____ 30 mill

B. Diff relig.

Ex: _____

C. _____ unfamiliar customs, foods, clothes, etc.

D. People scared imms would not share democ. values

Ex: _____

E. Amers. afraid of losing jobs

B Now watch or listen to Part 1 of the lecture. Fill in the blanks with the items below. Notice the use of telegraphic language, symbols, and abbreviations.

> Size of imm pop
> call imms cruel names
> prej vs Germans during WWI
> Reasons for prej
> prej vs Catholics + Jews
> 4 maj imm grps imm'ed to U.S. @ this time
> Diff langs

C Work with a partner and compare notes. Then use your notes to retell the information in Part 1 of the lecture.

1 Guessing vocabulary from context Ⓥ

A The following items contain important vocabulary from Part 2 of the lecture. Work with a partner. Using the context and your knowledge of related words, take turns guessing the meanings of the words in **bold**.

_____ **1.** It was a time of great **expansion** in America.

_____ **2.** A lot of these new workers were immigrants who made many important and **lasting** contributions to the development of the country.

_____ **3.** They were good at farming and made important **improvements** to U.S. farming methods.

_____ **4.** [They] helped build the **infrastructure** of many American cities.

_____ **5.** Many were skilled workers, like **plumbers**.

_____ **6.** **There's no doubt** that [all these immigrants] made important contributions . . .

B Work with your partner. Match the vocabulary terms from Step A with their definitions. Write the letter of the definition below in the blank next to the sentence containing the correct term in Step A. Check your answers in a dictionary if necessary.

a. positive developments

b. continuing for a long time

c. people who build systems of pipes that carry water

d. It is certain

e. growth

f. basic systems for transportation, communication, and energy

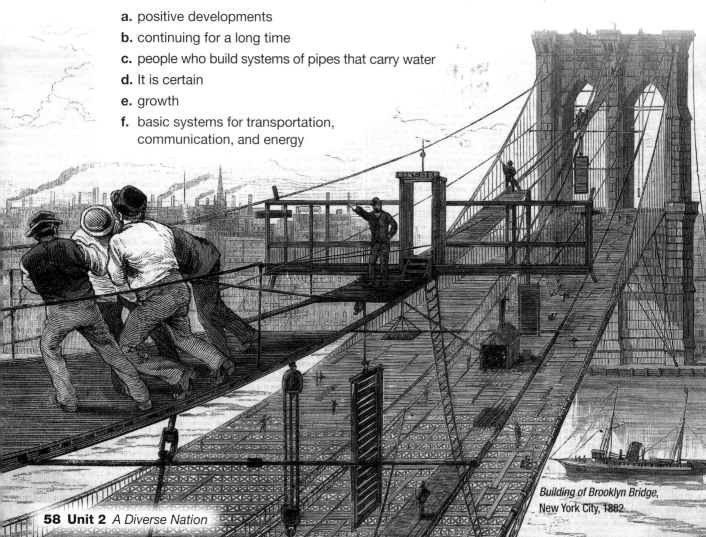

Building of Brooklyn Bridge, New York City, 1882

2 Organizing your notes in columns Ⓝ Ⓛ Ⓢ

Organizing your notes in columns allows you to separate different types of information. For example, you can use columns to separate main ideas and supporting details, or you can decide to separate different categories of information based on your own ideas.

A Look at these incomplete notes on Part 2 of the lecture. They are divided into two columns, "Immigrant Groups" and "Examples of Contributions," based on the note taker's ideas about how to take effective notes for this part of the lecture.

<u>Immigrants Make Lasting Contributions</u>

Immigrant Groups	Examples of Contributions
_____	→ _____ tailors, bakers, butchers
Irish	→ built _____
	inc. skilled wkrs, ex: _____
	+ unskilled, ex: _____
_____	→ _____ , entertainment, education,
	science, _____ industry
_____	→ built _____ , canals, _____
	buildings, and _____
All imms	→ contrib. to _____ and _____
	ex: _____ , _____ music, relig., lifestyles

B Now watch or listen to Part 2 of the lecture. Fill in the blanks with the missing information. Remember to use symbols, abbreviations, and telegraphic language.

C Work with a partner and compare notes. Then use your notes to retell the information in Part 2 of the lecture.

1 Answering multiple-choice questions Ⓢ

Professors and college instructors often give multiple-choice tests. Such tests are frequently graded using a computer. It is important to "bubble in" your responses correctly. Here are some examples:

Correct	Incorrect	Incorrect
●	⊖	⊖

A Read the questions and bubble in the correct answer according to the information in the lecture. You may use your notes.

1. Which word describes a common attitude toward immigrants at the turn of the century?	a. hostile b. welcoming c. puzzled d. inspired	○ a ○ b ○ c ○ d
2. How did many Americans view the immigrants?	a. as welcome contributors b. as a threat to the workers c. as skilled competitors d. as new friends	○ a ○ b ○ c ○ d
3. Which of the following is not given as a reason for prejudice against immigrants during this period?	a. The newcomers adjusted quickly. b. They spoke other languages. c. Their customs were different. d. They had different religions.	○ a ○ b ○ c ○ d
4. What was the major religion in the United States at this time?	a. Judaism b. Protestantism c. Catholicism d. none	○ a ○ b ○ c ○ d
5. What was true about the newcomers?	a. They contributed to the economy. b. They adopted Americans' lifestyles. c. They spoke only to each other. d. They learned English quickly.	○ a ○ b ○ c ○ d
6. Why were there many new jobs in America?	a. because of World War I b. because of foreign immigration c. because of the growth of industry d. because of World War II	○ a ○ b ○ c ○ d

B Work with a partner and compare answers.

2 Personalizing the topic Ⓢ

A Read the statements below and mark your opinion on the line.

1. When people move to a new country, they change that country in very important ways.

| Strongly agree | Agree | Not sure | Disagree | Strongly disagree |

2. It is easy to understand why there is often prejudice toward new immigrant groups.

| Strongly agree | Agree | Not sure | Disagree | Strongly disagree |

3. The biggest difficulty new immigrants face is loneliness.

| Strongly agree | Agree | Not sure | Disagree | Strongly disagree |

B Now work with a small group. Explain your responses to your classmates.

Chapter 4
Diversity in the United States Today

Look at the photo and then answer the questions with a partner.

1. Who are the people in the photo, and what are they doing?

2. What do you think their new life in the United States will be like? What are some of the challenges they are likely to face?

1 Getting Started

In this section, you are going to read about immigration to the United States from the second half of the twentieth century until the present. You will also hear statistics about this immigration and examine graphs about recent immigrants' countries of origin.

1 Reading and thinking about the topic Ⓥ Ⓢ

A Read the following passage.

> In 1965, there was a major change in U.S. immigration laws, and the number of people allowed to come into the United States began to increase. The pattern of immigration also changed. In the first half of the twentieth century, the majority of immigrants came from Europe. Since 1965, most immigrants have come from Latin America and Asia. Nowadays, they arrive from countries such as Mexico, China, and India, and from the Caribbean and eastern Europe. With so many ethnic groups, religions, and races, the United States is now one of the most diverse nations on earth.
>
> Economic opportunity and political freedom are still the main reasons for immigration to this country, but other factors are important, too. Americans' acceptance of diversity, better educational opportunities, and the existence of health care are other reasons why immigrants choose to make the United States their home.

Today's immigrants differ from one another in many ways. For example, some come to join their families, while others leave their families behind. Some immigrants are poor, uneducated workers, and others are middle-class professionals. After arriving in the United States, some make a lot of money, while others remain poor. Furthermore, there are differences in the way immigrants adapt to American society. Some adapt completely to the new culture and think of themselves as *American*. Others feel that they are a combination of both their original and new cultures. These immigrants sometimes call themselves "hyphenated Americans" (for example, *Mexican-American* or *Chinese-American*). Still others keep their original culture for their whole life.

B Answer the following questions according to the information in the passage.

1. How have immigration patterns to the United States changed since 1965?

2. Why do immigrants continue to come to America?

3. In what ways are immigrants different from each other?

C Read these questions and share your answers with a partner.

1. Do you know any people who have immigrated to the United States since 1965? Why did they immigrate? Have they successfully adapted to American society?

2. Why do you think immigrants sometimes adapt in different ways?

2 Listening for percentages and fractions

Percentages and fractions are commonly used in academic courses. They can be used for different purposes, such as explaining a graph or giving an example.

To express percentages, just add *percent* to a number. For example:

"1%" is said as *one percent.*
"3%" is said as *three percent.*
"13%" is said as *thirteen percent.*
"30%" is said as *thirty percent.*
"32%" is said as *thirty-two percent.*
"100%" is said as *one hundred percent.*

Fractions are expressed in the following ways:

"1/2" is said as *half* or *one-half* or *a half.*
"1/3" is said as *one-third* or *a third.*
"1/4" is said as *one-quarter* or *one-fourth* or *a quarter* or *a fourth.*
"3/4" is said as *three-quarters* or *three-fourths.*

A Study the three pie charts below. They show legal immigration to the United States in the twentieth century.

Legal Immigration to the United States

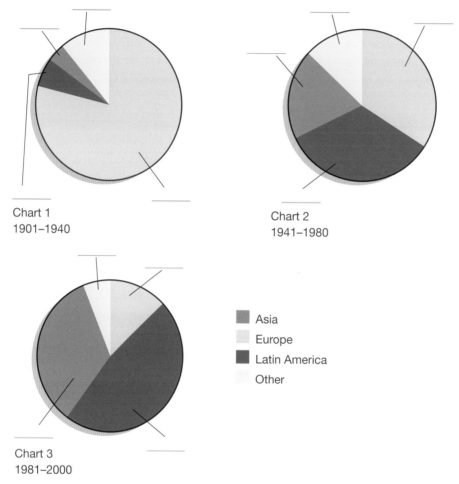

Chart 1
1901–1940

Chart 2
1941–1980

Chart 3
1981–2000

- Asia
- Europe
- Latin America
- Other

Source: **Immigration and Naturalization Service**

B Discuss these questions about the pie charts with a partner.

1. Which time periods are shown?
2. Which parts of the world are included?
3. What percentages or fractions do you predict you might hear?

C Listen to a description of twentieth-century immigration patterns. As you listen, fill in the blanks next to each pie chart with the percentages you hear.

D Work with a partner and compare your answers. Then discuss the following questions.

1. Since 1901, what has happened to the percentage of immigrants from Europe, Latin America, and Asia?
2. What fraction or percentage of immigrants came from Europe, Latin America, Asia, and other places between 1981 and 2000?
3. How do you think immigration patterns might change in the future? Why?

2 Real-Life Voices

In this section, you will hear interviews with six immigrants to the United States. First, Agustín, Nadezhda, and Chao will discuss their reasons for coming to the United States. Then Mateo, Minsoo, and Abdoul-Aziz will talk about adapting to life in this country.

BEFORE THE INTERVIEWS

1 Sharing your opinion Ⓢ

A Imagine that you are an immigrant to the United States. What were your reasons for coming to this country? Mark each item below as: 1 (very important), 2 (important), or 3 (not very important).

_____ The opportunity to make money   _____ Equal rights for women

_____ A good health-care system   _____ A democratic government

_____ A good educational system   _____ A safe place to raise children

_____ A diverse culture   _____ Other (your own ideas)

B Work in small groups. Discuss your responses in Step A.

2 Building background knowledge on the topic Ⓥ Ⓢ

A Read the following passage.

> The organization Public Agenda interviewed more than 1,000 immigrants to the United States from about 100 countries. It asked the immigrants if they agreed with the following statements:
>
> _____ 1. I have become an American.
>
> _____ 2. I act like an American outside, but at home I keep my own culture and traditions.
>
> _____ 3. I phone my family or friends in my home country a few times a month.
>
> _____ 4. My children [under 18] probably will not want to return to my country to live.
>
> _____ 5. The most important thing about living in the United States is having freedom to live my life the way I choose.
>
> _____ 6. Speaking English is the key to success in America.
>
> _____ 7. I would come to America again if I could go back in time.

B Work with a partner. From the list below, guess the percentage of immigrants who agreed with the statements above. Write the letters of your answers in the corresponding lines in step A.

a. 80   **b.** 42   **c.** 41   **d.** 59   **e.** 70   **f.** 40   **g.** 87

C Check your answers to Step B at the bottom of this page. Then discuss them with a partner.

1 Examining vocabulary in context Ⓥ

Here are some words and phrases from the interview with Agustín, Nadezhda, and Chao, printed in **bold** and given in the context in which you will hear them. They are followed by definitions.

I was washing dishes, but I didn't want to **get stuck** doing that: *do something forever*

We're often **in contact**. I always send money and **presents** back home: *We communicate often. / gifts*

I **made a sacrifice** for my children: *gave up something that was important to me*

I want to become a **physician's assistant**: *a person trained to help a doctor*

I work in a **tofu** factory: *soybean cake (a common food in parts of Asia)*

I'm studying to make my dream **come true**: *happen, become real*

2 Listening for specific information Ⓛ Ⓝ Ⓢ

A Look at the chart below and notice the information you need to listen for in the interview with Agustín, Nadezhda, and Chao.

	Agustín	Nadezhda	Chao
Country of origin			
Length of time in the U.S.			
Reason(s) for coming			
Difficulties in the beginning			
Life now			

🔊 **B** Listen to the interview and fill in the chart with the information you hear.

C Work with a partner and compare answers. Then discuss the following questions.

1. How are the speakers' experiences similar? How are they different?
2. What were the speakers' most challenging experiences?

1 Examining vocabulary in context Ⓥ

Here are some words and phrases from the interview printed in **bold** and given in the context in which you will hear them. They are followed by definitions.

> I'm a combination of two cultures . . . That's kind of like being a **hybrid**: *a thing made by combining parts from two different sources*

> Whenever **I step outside the door**, I **step** into a different world: *leave my house / walk*

> I'm constantly going **back and forth** between the two cultures: *from one to the other*

> I'm **not used to** giving my opinion in class: *not something I usually do, not a habit*

> . . . I'm **absorbing** American culture fast: *getting familiar with, taking in*

> Isn't it hard for you to **keep switching** languages?: *change all the time*

> Am I a **mixture** of both?: *a combination*

> My mother says I'm not as **formal** as I used to be: *correct, serious, extremely polite*

2 Listening for specific information Ⓛ Ⓝ Ⓢ

A Before you listen to the interview, read the paragraphs summarizing the conversation with Mateo, Minsoo, and Abdoul-Aziz. Predict the kind of information you need to listen for.

Mateo's family is from (1) _____ , but he grew up in (2) _____ . He describes himself as a (3) _____ , which in his case is a combination of two cultures. He says he is (4) _____ on the outside and (5) _____ inside. At home, he always speaks (6) _____ , listens to (7) _____ , and eats (8) _____ food. When he goes outside, he says he feels as if he is stepping into a different (9) _____ , so he is constantly going (10) _____ between two cultures.

Minsoo is from (1) _____ , and she came to the United States five years ago. At home, she speaks (2) _____ . She only speaks English at (3) _____ and in college. It is difficult for her at college, because she is not used to giving her (4) _____ in class. Minsoo feels that she is half (5) _____ and half American, but she says she is (6) _____ American culture fast.

Abdoul-Aziz grew up in (1) _____ and came to the United States as an (2) _____ . He speaks three languages: (3) _____ at work and school, (4) _____ with some of his friends, and Hausa, an (5) _____ language, with (6) _____ . He says it is hard to keep (7) _____ languages because it feels like he is constantly changing his (8) _____ . He often asks himself: Am I Nigerian? Am I American? Or am I a (9) _____ of both?

🔊 **B** Listen to the interview. As you listen, fill in the blanks in the paragraphs. Then work with a partner and compare answers.

C Work with a partner. Choose two people from the interview and role-play a conversation between them. You can use questions like these to begin.

    1. Why did you come to the United States?

    2. What exciting, frightening, or difficult experience did you have when you first arrived?

    3. Do you miss your home country? If so, in what ways?

    4. Do you think of yourself as an American?

3 Listening for stressed words Ⓛ Ⓢ

A Read the sentences below.

Excerpt One

Mateo is explaining how he acts inside and outside his house. The word he stresses is

    a. constantly.   **b.** between.   **c.** cultures.

Excerpt Two

Minsoo is explaining the reason why she immigrated to the U.S. The word she stresses is

    a. here.   **b.** opportunities.   **c.** women.

Excerpt Three

Abdoul-Aziz is discussing the ways he has changed since he immigrated. The word he stresses is

    a. mother.   **b.** formal.   **c.** used.

◄⑴ **B** Now listen to the excerpts and circle the word that the interviewees stress. Compare your responses with a partner.

AFTER THE INTERVIEWS

Discussing your experience Ⓢ

Work with a partner. Ask and answer the chain of questions in the chart below. Use examples and stories to tell about your experiences.

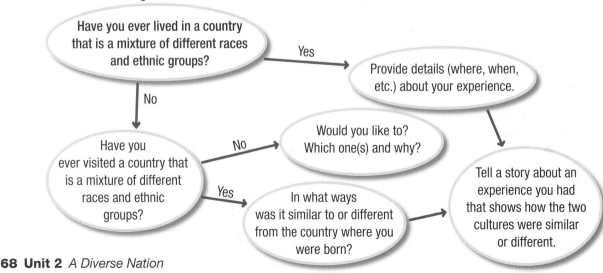

Begin here:

Have you ever lived in a country that is a mixture of different races and ethnic groups?

— Yes → Provide details (where, when, etc.) about your experience.

No ↓

Have you ever visited a country that is a mixture of different races and ethnic groups?

— No → Would you like to? Which one(s) and why?

Yes → In what ways was it similar to or different from the country where you were born?

→ Tell a story about an experience you had that shows how the two cultures were similar or different.

3 In Your Own Voice

When you think of American food, holidays, customs, and music, what do you think of? Hot dogs and hamburgers? Thanksgiving and Labor Day? Rock 'n' roll and R & B? In fact, food, holiday celebrations, and music are extremely varied because U.S. culture is so diverse. In this section, you will discuss elements of American culture that were originally brought to the country by an immigrant group.

A Work with a partner. Read the list of dishes below and match each one with the country or region it originally came from.

c	**1.** sushi	**a.** Jamaica
d	**2.** tacos	**b.** China
e	**3.** hummus	**c.** Japan
i	**4.** gyros	**d.** Mexico
j	**5.** samosas	**e.** Middle East
a	**6.** ackee	**f.** eastern Europe
b	**7.** eggdrop soup	**g.** Italy
f	**8.** matzo ball soup	**h.** Germany
g	**9.** pizza	**i.** Greece
h	**10.** hot dogs	**j.** India

B Choose one of the dishes from Step A and answer the questions. Use a dictionary or online resource to find the information, or ask a classmate.

1. What country did the dish you chose come from originally?

2. What ingredients does it contain?

3. How do you prepare it?

4. What does it look like when it is finished?

5. What other foods can you eat with it?

C Read the list of holidays that are celebrated in the United States. Match each item with its description. Then tell your partner what you know about these holidays.

Holiday or celebration

_____ **1.** Three Kings Day

_____ **2.** Spring Festival

_____ **3.** Mardi Gras

_____ **4.** Rosh Hashanah

_____ **5.** St. Patrick's Day

_____ **6.** Cinco de Mayo

_____ **7.** Ramadan

_____ **8.** Diwali

_____ **9.** Kwanzaa

Descriptions

a. month-long religious holiday celebrated among Muslims

b. Catholic holiday when parents give children gifts

c. carnival that often involves wearing costumes and masks

d. cultural and religious holiday celebrated by the Irish community

e. Indian festival of lights

f. week-long celebration of African-American history and culture

g. Jewish New Year

h. Chinese New Year

i. celebration of Mexican heritage and pride

D Read the list below. It shows different kinds of music that are popular in the United States. As a class, share what you know about the origins and popularity of these types of music.

- bachata
- bluegrass
- Celtic
- country and western
- gospel
- jazz
- merengue
- reggaeton
- salsa

4 Academic Listening and Note Taking

In this section, you will hear and take notes on a two-part lecture given by Betty Jordan, a professor of U.S. history. The title of her lecture is "Recent Immigrants and Today's United States." Professor Jordan will talk about models, or metaphors, for describing America's diverse immigrant society. She will also discuss *transnationalism*, a word that describes recent immigrants' continuing relationships with their home countries.

BEFORE THE LECTURE

1 Previewing the topic ⓢ

A Work with a partner. Look at the pictures that the speaker will include in her PowerPoint presentation. What do these pictures show? Write your answers on the lines.

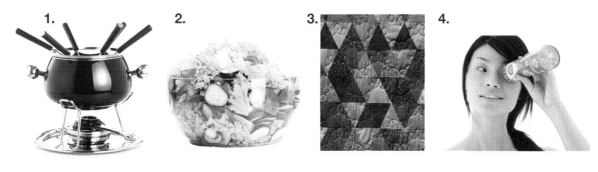

1. _____ 2. _____ 3. _____ 4. _____

B Imagine that you have recently immigrated to another country. Look at the activities below and check (✓) the column that describes how often you would do each one.

I would . . .	Very often	Often	Sometimes	Almost never
phone people in my home country.				
communicate online with family and friends back home.				
celebrate traditional holidays from my home country.				
cook food from my home country.				
follow sports events in my home country.				
speak my native language with my children.				
speak my native language with other people from my home country.				
practice my religion.				
send money to people in my home country.				
visit my home country.				

C Work in small groups and discuss these questions: What kind of immigrant would you be, based on your answers in Step B? Would you completely adapt to your new culture, adapt in some ways but not others, or not adapt at all?

2 Listening for definitions

Good lecturers usually define important terms and difficult vocabulary. Definitions often follow this formula:

X (word being defined) *is a* (category or type of something) *that/who/where* (details).

Here are some examples.

- **An immigrant** *is a person who goes to live in another country.*
- **Transnationalism** *is a word that describes recent immigrants' relationships with their home countries.*

A Work with a partner to complete the sentences. Use words and expressions from the chart to fill in the blank spaces.

First blank space	Second blank space
metaphor	tube
melting pot	cover for a bed
salad	figure of speech
patchwork quilt	dish
kaleidoscope	metal container

1. A _____ is a _____ that compares one thing to another.
2. A _____ is a _____ that is used to turn solids into liquids.
3. A _____ is a _____ that is made from different vegetables.
4. A _____ is a _____ that is made from pieces of cloth.
5. A _____ is a _____ that shows complex, changing patterns.

 B Watch or listen to the excerpts and check your answers.

1 Guessing vocabulary from context Ⓥ

A The following items contain important vocabulary from Part 1 of the lecture. Work with a partner. Using the context and your knowledge of related words, take turns guessing the meanings of the words in **bold**.

_____ 1. . . . the ingredients all **melt** together and become something new.

_____ 2. A fondue . . . [is] a dish from Switzerland that has cheese and other **ingredients**.

_____ 3. . . . many immigrants keep parts of their own cultural **identity**.

_____ 4. They may **celebrate** their own traditional holidays.

_____ 5. They usually marry someone from their own race – their own **ethnic** group.

_____ 6. . . . pieces of colorful cloth **sewn** together.

_____ 7. This is the metaphor I like best because it's very **dynamic**.

_____ 8. . . . it shows America as a beautiful picture – a **multiracial**, **multiethnic**, **multicultural** society that is always changing.

B Work with your partner. Match the vocabulary terms with their definitions by writing the letter of each definition below in the blank next to the sentence containing the correct term in Step A. Check your answers in a dictionary if necessary.

a. composed of many races, ethnic groups, and cultures

b. always moving or changing

c. items of food that are used in cooking or preparing a dish

d. people's idea of who they are and what makes them special

e. enjoy a special event, such as a holiday, by eating and drinking, playing special music, or participating in traditional activities

f. made by sewing, using a needle and thread

g. relating to a particular race, nationality, or culture

h. change from a solid to a liquid form because they are heated

2 Reviewing and revising notes ⓝ ⓛ

It is common for lecturers to hand out a copy of their PowerPoint presentation that includes the graphics but leaves space for you to take notes. This often makes it easier for listeners to concentrate and to organize their notes quickly. For example, the class hears: *Over the years, historians and writers have used different metaphors to try to describe this complex American culture. What I'd like to do today is, first describe four of those metaphors to you, and then, in the second part of the lecture, talk about* **transnationalism**. *Transnationalism is a word that describes the relationship that recent immigrants continue to have with their home countries.* While listening, students receive the following handout:

A Look at this handout from Part 1 of the lecture.

B Here is how a student took notes on the slide. Look at the notes.
With a partner, try to put the notes into complete sentences.

C Look at these notes for the other slides in Part 1 of the lecture. Notice how the note taker has used numbers to identify and organize the main ideas. Predict the information you will need to listen for.

The United States Today:

A Racial and Ethnic Melting Pot?

1. Melting pot = metal container used for turning solids into liquid
2. Ingredients melt together & become s't new, e.g., fondue
3. Acc to metaphor, imms to U.S. would lose separate ID & mix together
4. Problem w/metaphor: doesn't describe today's reality, i.e., many imms aren't accepted
5. Many imms keep parts of own ID – lang, traditions, marry from same ethnic grp, never say they are American.

The "Salad Bowl" Metaphor

Salad bowl metaphor
1. Salad = _____
2. Metaphor represents America as _____
3. _____
4. _____
5. _____

The "Quilt" Metaphor

The "Kaleidoscope" Metaphor

D Now watch or listen to Part 1 of the lecture and complete the notes on page 75.

E Work with a partner and compare notes. Use them to retell the information in Part 1.

F Think of your own metaphor for American society and explain it to your partner by completing the following sentence:

America is a(n) _____ *because . . .*

1 Guessing vocabulary from context Ⓥ

A The following book review contains important vocabulary from Part 2 of the lecture. Work with a partner. Using the context and your knowledge of related words, take turns guessing the meanings of the words in **bold**.

A New Vision, the recent book published about America's diverse ethnic mix, examines the way that today's immigrants view their cultural identity. Today, of course, there are many factors that make it possible for people to (1) **maintain** a strong relationship with their countries of origin. Air travel has become more convenient, so immigrants can easily return to their (2) **homeland**. Even if traveling home is not possible, the (3) **ease** with which you can now make cheap phone calls makes communication more frequent. Since communication technology has (4) **advanced**, people can chat online with loved ones back home on a daily or weekly basis. The book examines the phenomenon of *transnationalism,* too, giving examples of immigrants who (5) **own** land or homes in their country of origin. The most interesting part of the book is its examination of the way in which immigrants in the early 21st century are becoming part of (6) **mainstream** American society. This is a must-read for anyone interested in today's multicultural society.

B Work with your partner. Match the vocabulary terms from Step A with their definitions below. Write the word on the line. Check your answers in a dictionary if necessary.

a. made progress _____

b. have, possess _____

c. keep, have _____

d. without difficulty _____

e. country of origin, home country _____

f. common, part of the majority _____

2 Using bullets to organize your notes Ⓝ Ⓛ Ⓢ

Bullets are a useful technique for marking lists of details. You can use them with numbers or instead of numbers. For example, you hear:

Now, why do you think immigrants today have a closer relationship with their home countries than they did in the past? Well, there are different factors that make this possible, like ease of travel and technology.

Your notes could look like this:

Imm's have close r'ship w/home countries – why?
- travel
- technology

A Look at these notes on Part 2 of the lecture and notice how the note taker has used bullets to help identify and organize the main ideas and examples.

Transnationalism = _____
_____

Examples of transnationalism:
- imms may own _____
- send _____
- support _____
- travel _____
- get involved in _____

The world is getting smaller and smaller...

Ways that immigrants stay connected:
- _____
- _____
- _____

🔊 **B** Now watch or listen to Part 2 of the lecture and complete the notes.

📹 **C** Work with a partner and compare your notes. Use them to retell the information in Part 2.

Sharing your opinion Ⓢ

A Read the postcards that Jo Ann, who is visiting the United States, sent to her friend Sharon in their hometown of Basildon, Essex County, England.

Sharon – Just a quick note to tell you I've arrived safely in Southern California. I like my college a lot, and I've got a great roommate, Maria (she's from New Mexico). What's amazing is how much there is to do here even though the town is small. There's a Native American arts center near the college, and right on my block there's a Russian dance studio where they give free performances Friday nights. Plus lots of fun places to eat – last night a few of us went to a terrific Turkish restaurant that has live music.

Gotta go! Will try to write more later.

Hugs and kisses,

Jo Ann

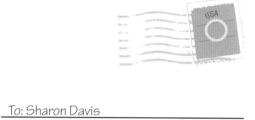

To: Sharon Davis

P.O. Box 1904

Essex

5516 IZQ

UK

Hi Sharon,

I'm having a great time in New York! Too bad spring break is so short. Can you believe that there's a Chinese, a Jamaican, a Lebanese, a Mexican, an Italian, and a Japanese restaurant all on the same street?? And the choice of music is amazing: jazz, swing, classical, rock, hip-hop. I've never seen anything like it! Yesterday, Maria and I went to Queens – it's just across the East River – and we walked through an Indian neighborhood and then a Mexican one. And then we went to a museum that had all kinds of contemporary art. I'm taking lots of photos. Will send them as soon as I get back to CA.

Love—

Jo Ann

To: Sharon Davis

P.O. Box 1904

Essex

5516 IZQ

UK

B Discuss the following questions with a partner.

1. Where is Jo Ann, and what is she doing?

2. What does her description tell you about life in the United States? How does it support what you have learned in this unit?

Unit 2 Academic Vocabulary Review

This section reviews the vocabulary from Chapters 3 and 4. For a complete list all of the Academic Word List words in this book, see the Appendix on page 182.

A Read the paragraphs and fill in the blanks with a form of the numbered words. If you are using a noun, be sure to use the singular or plural form correctly. If you are using a verb, make sure to check it is in the right tense and form. You will not use all of the words given.

1. adaptation (n), adapt (v)   **3.** complexity (n), complex (adj)

2. communication (n), communicate (v)

Just as adult immigrants often find it hard to (a) _____ to life in a new country, children do, too. Learning new customs may seem easy, but actually it is difficult to understand the (b) _____ of many of the customs we take for granted. For example, why do many Americans eat turkey at Thanksgiving? Why do some American children hunt for eggs at Easter? Explaining this to a child can be quite challenging.

In addition, if children have problems (c) _____ their ideas in English, they are likely to find it hard to fit in with their new environment, at least at first. Luckily, the period of (d) _____ tends to be shorter for children than for adults.

4. contribution (n), contribute (v)   **6.** diversity (n), diverse (adj)

5. culture (n), cultural (adj)

Immigration to the United States at the beginning of the 21st century is at an all-time high. The country is now more (e) _____ than it has ever been, with minority populations rising quickly in almost every state. This (f) _____ makes the U.S. a very exciting place to live.

For example, immigrants bring different (g) _____ traditions with them. It is often said that salsa, the spicy dip that came originally from Mexico, is now more popular than ketchup, and reggaeton is certainly popular among U.S. teenagers. Of course, in addition to new food and music, immigrants also make other important (h) _____ to the country.

7. economy (n), economic (adj)   **9.** ethnicity (n), ethnic (adj)

8. energy (n), energetic (adj)

Visitors to large American cities such as Los Angeles, Chicago, or New York often visit (i) _____ neighborhoods such as Little Italy, Little Tokyo, or Chinatown if they have a lot of (j) _____ and are prepared to spend a long time on their feet. These neighborhoods are wonderful. They are busy, (k) _____ centers of commerce, art, and culture. Indeed, tourism is very important for the (l) _____ development of these neighborhoods.

10. expansion (n), expanded (v)

11. identity (n), identify (v)

12. involvement (n), involve (v)

Most elementary and middle schools are aware of the importance of (m) _____ parents in daily activities in the classroom. Therefore, teachers try to maximize the (n) _____ of parents by inviting them to class trips and special celebrations. One school in New Jersey has (o) _____ this idea by inviting immigrant parents into the classroom to teach the children about the customs and traditions of their native countries. The principal said: "When we looked at the class records, we were able to (p) _____ parents from 10 different countries. We contacted them, and they all came in and spoke to the children. It was a great success! The children were thrilled to be able to learn about each other's backgrounds, so I'm sure we will repeat this activity next year."

13. professional (n), professionally (adv)

14. survival (n), survive (v)

15. unique (adj), uniquely (adv)

A new novel, *Half and Half*, is about a young girl called Jocelyn whose parents are both from the West Indies. It offers a (q) _____ perspective on the pressures that many immigrants face.

Jocelyn's parents are (r) _____ actors who immigrated to the U.S. when she was a baby. However, when she is 16, the family moves back home. Jocelyn decides not to go with them. Will she be able to (s) _____ alone in the United States?

The novelist's own background is very similar to Jocelyn's, and that is why she is (t) _____ qualified to explain the conflict that her characters face in the story. Not surprisingly, *Half and Half* has quickly become a best-seller.

B Use the academic vocabulary from A above to answer the following questions in pairs or as a class.

Early Immigrants to the United States

1. Which groups came to the United States in the late nineteenth and early twentieth centuries?

2. What are "push" and "pull" factors, and how do they help to explain immigration?

Achievements and Difficulties of Immigrant Groups

3. What contributions did immigrants make to America?

4. What difficulties did they face?

Late Twentieth-Century Immigration to the United States

5. Which groups are coming to the United States today?

6. How does their experience compare with the experience of previous immigrant groups?

The Changing United States

7. What are some common metaphors to describe diversity in the United States?

8. What does *transnationalism* mean?

Oral Presentation

In academic courses, you will sometimes need to report on a project you have been assigned to complete outside of class. For this presentation, you will need to work in pairs, conduct interviews outside of class about immigration, and report on your findings.

1 Prepare your interview

What are the factors that make it difficult for people to move from one country to another? Work in a small group and fill in the mindmap with possible questions.

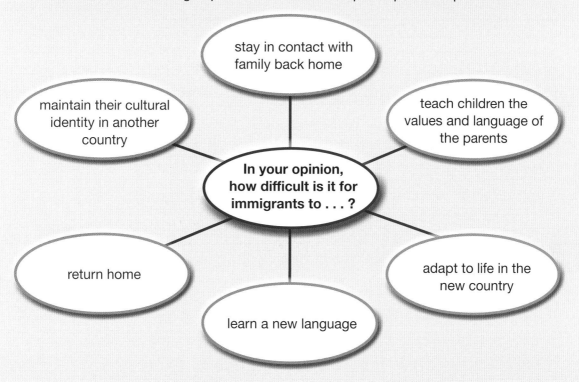

2 Conduct your interview

In pairs, interview at least two people outside of class. If possible, your interviewees should be immigrants, children of immigrants, or people who know someone who has immigrated.

Remember to explain why you are asking your questions and to thank your interviewees.

3 Organize your presentation

After the interviews, prepare a 3-minute summary of your findings.
You should plan to explain who you spoke to and what that person said.

1 Introduce your presentation

Write the questions on the board so that your audience can focus on your explanation of the interviewees' answers.

2 Make eye contact

Look up at your audience and stand up straight. Explain the most interesting ideas your interviewees shared. Make sure you include any examples they gave.

3 Take turns

Make sure each person has enough time to share his or her report.

AFTER THE PRESENTATION

Performing a peer-assessment

In a group, answer the questions below. Discuss your presentations and give each other respectful suggestions about how to improve.

Did you . . .

- [ ] accurately communicate what the interviewees said?
- [ ] speak clearly and make eye contact?
- [ ] take turns and share the time evenly?
- [ ] take responsibility for your part of the project?

Unit 3
The Struggle for Equality

In this unit, you will learn about the struggle for equality in the United States. Equality was an important ideal for the men who founded the country, but in the early days of U.S. history, not everyone had the same rights or opportunities (for example, only white men who owned property could vote). Chapter 5 is about political movements in the nineteenth and twentieth centuries that led to greater equality. You will hear interviews with two people who experienced discrimination, and a lecture on the civil rights movement and the women's movement. Chapter 6 discusses progress since the 1960s. You will listen to people talk about groups that have taken steps toward greater equality, and you will hear a lecture about laws that have advanced America's struggle for equality.

Contents

In Unit 3, you will listen to and speak about the following topics.

Chapter 5 The Struggle Begins	Chapter 6 The Struggle Continues
Interview 1 A Personal Encounter with Segregation **Interview 2** An Inspiring Time **Lecture** The Civil Rights Movement and the Women's Movement	**Interview 1** Issues of Inequality **Interview 2** Working with the Blind **Lecture** Two Important Laws in the Struggle for Equality

Skills

In Unit 3, you will practice the following skills.

(L) Listening Skills

Listening for answers to *Wh-* questions
Listening for specific information
Listening for stressed words
Listening for guiding questions
Listening for main ideas
Listening for tone of voice
Listening for signal words and phrases

(S) Speaking Skills

Sharing your opinion
Drawing inferences
Reviewing your notes after a lecture
Thinking critically about the topic

(V) Vocabulary Skills

Building background knowledge on the topic
Reading and thinking about the topic
Examining vocabulary in context
Guessing vocabulary from context

(N) Note Taking Skills

Creating your own symbols and abbreviations
Organizing your notes in a chart
Indenting
Using an outline
Using your notes to make a time line

Learning Outcomes

Prepare and **deliver** a poster presentation on an individual who played a role in the struggle for equality

Chapter 5
The Struggle Begins

PARAMOUNT THEATRE
COLORED ENTRANCE
Enjoy Good Shows in Comfort

Look at the photograph and answer the questions with a partner.

1. The term *colored* was commonly used for African Americans until the 1960s. What does this photo tell you about the challenges African Americans faced at that time?

2. What changes have taken place since that time?

1 Getting Started

In this section, you will read some background information about the inequalities that African Americans and women have faced in the United States. As you read, you may notice that the terms *African Americans* and *blacks* are often used interchangeably.

1 Reading and thinking about the topic ⓥ ⓢ

A Read the following passage.

The American Civil War between the North and the South (1861–1865) ended in a major step forward in African Americans' struggle for equality. After the war, Congress passed the Thirteenth Amendment to the Constitution, which freed all slaves. A short time later, the Fourteenth Amendment was passed, which promised "equal protection of the law" to all citizens. And then in 1870, the Fifteenth Amendment gave African-American men the right to vote. However, in the following decades, so-called "Jim Crow"* laws in the South put limits on the newly won rights of black Americans. For example, blacks were not allowed to study in the same schools as whites, they were forced to sit at the back of buses, and they had to use separate bathrooms and water fountains. In 1954, the Supreme Court decided that segregation (the forced separation of the races) in public schools was unconstitutional, but it took many more years of struggle before the Jim Crow laws were completely reversed.

American women also began their struggle for equality around the time of the Civil War. Although many women had supported freeing the slaves and giving equal rights to blacks, they did not have many legal rights themselves. For example, they could not vote, they could not own land without their husband's permission, and they usually depended on their husbands or male relatives for economic support. It wasn't until 1920, under the Nineteenth Amendment, that women finally won the right to vote. During World War II (1939–1945), many women worked outside their homes for the first time. This was also an important step forward in their struggle for equal rights.

In the 1960s, both African Americans and women gained some important rights. The Equal Pay Act, a law passed in 1963, prohibited unequal pay for men and women in similar jobs at the same workplace. The Civil Rights Act, a law passed in 1964, made it illegal to discriminate against workers because of their race or gender.

B Answer the following questions according to the information in the passage.

1. Which events between the mid-nineteenth and mid-twentieth centuries led to greater equality for African Americans?
2. How did women's rights change during this time?
3. What laws were passed in the 1960s? How did they help blacks and women?

C Read these questions and share your answers with a partner.

1. What does equality mean to you?
2. Do you know of any laws that guarantee equal pay in other countries? Do you know when and why they were passed?

---

*"Jim Crow" was the name of a slave played by a white comedian in the early 1800s. Although he was poor and ignorant, Jim Crow was constantly smiling and dancing. He gave white people the impression that African Americans were happy as slaves.

2 Building background knowledge on the topic Ⓥ Ⓛ

A Work with a partner. Look at the photos and read the text that goes with them. Based on what you know about American history, circle the correct year.

_____ **a.** This is a picture of the Declaration of Independence, adopted on July 4, (*1776 / 1886*). It includes the famous phrase "We hold these truths to be self-evident, that all men are created equal."

_____ **b.** This picture shows an African American man drinking water at a segregated water fountain. Scenes like this were common in the South during the Jim Crow era, which lasted from about 1880 until the (*early 1900s /1960s*).

_____ **c.** This picture shows American women demonstrating for the right to vote. Women won this right in (*1850 / 1920*), when the U.S. Congress passed the Nineteenth Amendment.

_____ **d.** This picture shows African Americans protesting school segregation. Legal segregation of public schools ended in (*1954 / 1994*) in a Supreme Court case called *Brown versus Board of Education of Topeka*.

B Listen to information about the pictures. Fill in the blanks with the dates you hear. Then compare those dates with the dates in parentheses that you circled.

2 Real-Life Voices

In this section, you will hear two women tell stories about their experiences with inequality. First, you will listen to Cynthia, who is African American. Cynthia will talk about an event from her childhood, before the civil rights movement. Then you will hear Hilda, a retired teacher, talk about progress toward women's rights.

BEFORE THE INTERVIEWS

Building background knowledge on the topic Ⓥ Ⓢ

A From the 1880s until the 1960s, many southern American states were segregated. Read the following statements and guess whether they are true or false. Write *T* (true) or *F* (false) in the blanks. Then check your answers on page 91.

_____ **1. Alabama:** Restaurants would not serve whites and blacks in the same parts of the restaurant.

_____ **2. Florida:** Blacks were not allowed to marry whites.

_____ **3. Georgia:** Black children were not allowed to play ball games within 10 blocks of a white baseball team.

_____ **4. Mississippi:** A person who was one-quarter black could not marry a white person.

_____ **5. North Carolina:** A textbook used by a black child could not be used by a white child.

_____ **6. Oklahoma:** There were separate telephone booths for whites and blacks.

B Based on the statements above, list some of the activities that segregation affected (eating in a restaurant, getting married, etc.). Then choose the law that you think was most unfair and explain your reaction to the class.

C Until the women's movement in the 1960s, women did not have the same rights as men. Read the following statements and guess whether they are true or false. Write *T* (true) or *F* (false) in the blanks. Then check your answers on page 91.

_____ **1.** In the mid-1800s, only 55 percent of girls and women could read and write.

_____ **2.** In the late 1800s, the U.S. Supreme Court upheld a state law denying married women the right to become lawyers.

_____ **3.** In general, women could not become doctors until the late nineteenth century.

_____ **4.** Employers could refuse to give a job to a pregnant woman until the late 1970s.

_____ **5.** In 2008, many women earned as little as 58 cents for every dollar earned by men.

_____ **6.** In 2005, 14 out of 100 U.S. senators were women.

D Tell your classmates which fact about women surprised you the most.

1 Examining vocabulary in context Ⓥ

Here are some words and phrases from the interview with Cynthia printed in **bold** and given in the context in which you will hear them. They are followed by definitions.

[We'd take a trip] to **reconnect** with the family down there: *see them again*

Were you aware of segregation?: *Did you know about*

The owner . . . **grabbed me**: *took hold of me in a strong way*

He **swung me around**: *picked me up and turned me around*

I was really **startled**: *very surprised, shocked*

He couldn't **guarantee** our safety: *be absolutely sure to provide*

My father still doesn't want to talk about . . . how **helpless** he felt: *without power*

2 Listening for answers to *Wh-* questions Ⓛ Ⓝ

When speakers tell stories about events that happened to them, they often include the answers to *Wh-* questions.

- *Who* (was involved)?
- *What* (happened to them)?
- *When* (did the event happen)?
- *Where* (did it happen)?
- *Why* or *how* (did it happen)?

Listening for answers to these questions will help you understand the point the speaker is making.

A Before you listen to the interview, read the following *Wh-* questions about the experience Cynthia describes.

1. Who was Cynthia with when she had this experience?
2. What happened to her?
3. When did this experience take place?
4. Where was the family going?
5. Why was the event so frightening?

B Now listen to the interview and take notes on the answers to the questions in Step A.

C Compare your answers with a partner.

1 Examining vocabulary in context

Here are some words and phrases from the interview with Hilda printed in **bold** and given in the context in which you will hear them. They are followed by definitions.

Since I was born, there have been **incredible** changes: *unbelievable*

At least, that was the **stereotype**: *unfair, inaccurate generalization about a group of people*

You don't need a college education to change **diapers**: *babies' underclothes*

It took a while until I **realized** that I could do even better than that: *became aware*

It was **phenomenal**: *fantastic, wonderful*

Those kinds of **demands** opened my eyes: *strong requests*

I can get an education and **make something of myself**: *become successful*

Back then, it was a **big deal**: *something important*

2 Listening for specific information ⓛ ⓥ ⓢ

A Read the questions below before you listen to the interview with Hilda.

1. How old is Hilda?
   a. in her 50s
   b. in her 60s
   c. in her 70s
2. In what decade did Hilda go to high school?
   a. the 1940s
   b. the 1950s
   c. the 1960s
3. How many children did the "typical" American family have at that time?
   a. one
   b. two or three
   c. four or more
4. Who went to college in Hilda's family?
   a. her father
   b. her mother
   c. her brother

5. Why weren't women expected to go to college?
   a. They weren't considered as smart as men.
   b. They had to go out to work.
   c. They were expected to stay at home.
6. What was Hilda's dream?
   a. to be a secretary
   b. to go to college
   c. to be a housewife
7. What did Hilda do after the 1965 women's demonstration in Chicago?
   a. She married her brother's friend.
   b. She went to college.
   c. She got her first job.
8. What does Hilda think of the situation of women today?
   a. It has not changed.
   b. It is better than before.
   c. It is worse than ever.

B Now listen to the interview and circle the correct answer to each question in Step A.

C Work with a partner and check your answers. Then compare Hilda's life with the life of a woman you know who is about the same age as Hilda.

3 Listening for stressed words 🅛 🅢

A Listen again to excerpts from the interview. Circle the correct answers.

Excerpt One

Hilda is talking about changes in society. She says, "Life is very different for women these days."

1. Which word does she stress?

a. very

b. women

2. Which statement is true?

c. Hilda believes that life has changed more for women than it has for men.

d. Hilda believes that life is extremely different from the way it was in the past.

Excerpt Two

Hilda is discussing her family's attitude toward education. She says, "There was never any discussion of me going to college."

3. Which word does she stress?

a. never

b. me

4. Which statement is true?

c. Hilda's family did not talk about college in front of her.

d. Hilda's family did not consider the possibility of their daughter attending college.

Excerpt Three

Hilda is discussing her feelings. She says, "I thought 'I can get an education and make something of myself.'"

5. Which word does she stress?

a. can

b. education

6. Which statement is true?

c. Hilda realized that education was the only way to be successful in life.

d. Hilda began to see new opportunities for herself.

B Compare your responses with a partner.

Step C: All statements are true.
Step A: 1. T, 2. T, 3. F (2 blocks, not 10), 4. F (one-eighth, not one-quarter), 5. T, 6. T
Answers to "Building background knowledge on the topic," page 88

1 Sharing your opinion ⑤

In a small group, share your responses to the following questions.

1. Have you ever been to a political demonstration or seen one on TV? What was it for, and what was its impact?

2. Have you ever had an experience like Hilda's that "opened your eyes" and made you see things in a different way? What happened?

3. Hilda described some stereotypes about women. What are some stereotypes about men? In what way are the stereotypes true or not true?

2 Drawing inferences ⑤

Drawing inferences, sometimes called "reading between the lines," means understanding information that speakers do not say directly. In order to draw inferences, you must use your background knowledge, the speaker's tone of voice, and context clues to reach logical conclusions.

A Work with a partner and discuss the following inference questions.

1. How did Cynthia and her family members probably feel after the experience at the gas station?

2. Why do you think Cynthia's father did not want to discuss the experience?

3. How do you think Hilda's family felt about her career choices?

4. How do you think Hilda's life would be different if she were a young woman today?

B Imagine that it is the day after Cynthia's experience at the gas station or that it is the day after Hilda's experience at the women's demonstration. Write an imaginary diary entry by either Cynthia or Hilda. Then read your diary entry to a partner or a small group. (Use your own paper if you need more space.)

3 In Your Own Voice

In this section, you will read some information about celebrations that honor different groups. Then you will share what you have learned with other class members.

Building background knowledge on the topic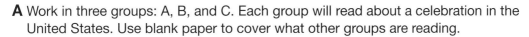

A Work in three groups: A, B, and C. Each group will read about a celebration in the United States. Use blank paper to cover what other groups are reading.

Group A: Black History Month. Read the information below.

Group B: Hispanic Heritage Month. Read the information at the top of page 94.

Group C: Women's History Month. Read the information at the bottom of page 94.

B As you read, answer these questions.

1. What is this celebration about, and when did it begin?
2. What month is the celebration, and why is it held then?
3. What are some important themes and slogans of the celebration?

Group A: Black History Month

Black History Month celebrates important events and promotes the study of African American history. In 1926, a special week was established to honor black Americans, but a month-long celebration has existed since 1970.

Black History Month takes place in February, the month that Abraham Lincoln and Frederick Douglass were born. Lincoln and Douglass are famous Americans who fought to end slavery.

Themes in Black History month include the struggle for equality, the contributions of black Americans, and the community's future hopes. Some slogans are:

- Injustice for some is injustice for all.
- Freedom is never given: It is won.
- Black history is American history.
- Fight for what's right, every day and night.

Rosa Parks

Thurgood Marshall

Martin Luther King, Jr.

Group B: Hispanic Heritage Month

Hispanic Heritage Month celebrates the history and contributions of Hispanics in the United States. The month-long celebration began in 1988 although a week-long celebration of Hispanics in the United States started in 1968.

Hispanic Heritage Month takes place every year from mid-September to mid-October. September and October are months when many Latin American countries first became independent, and October 12 is Columbus Day, the day Christopher Columbus arrived in the Americas.

Hispanic Heritage Month focuses on themes such as the diversity of the Hispanic population, the hopes of Latinos in the United States, and prominent leaders in the community. Some slogans are:

- Many backgrounds, many stories . . . one American spirit
- Renewing the American Dream
- Latino leaders in a global society
- ¡Sí, se puede! (Yes, we can!)

Sonia Sotomayor

Isabel Allende

César Chávez

Group C: Women's History Month

Women's History Month honors the history and contributions of women. This celebration began in 1987, and it happens in countries all over the world.

Women's History Month takes place every year in March. March is when International Women's Day is celebrated. This important celebration began in 1911.

Themes in Women's History month include women's contributions to society, women's leadership, and women's success in science and technology. Some slogans are:

- Women's education – women's empowerment
- Women taking the lead to save our planet
- Women inspiring innovation through imagination
- Women: builders of communities and dreams

Susan B. Anthony

Eleanor Roosevelt

Elizabeth Cady Stanton

C Work in new groups of three students, one from Group A, one from Group B, and one from Group C. Take turns explaining your answers to the questions above.

4 Academic Listening and Note Taking

In this section, you will hear and take notes on a two-part lecture given by Julia Smith, a professor of sociology. The title of her lecture is "The Civil Rights Movement and the Women's Movement." Professor Smith will discuss these two mid-twentieth-century political movements and explain how they changed the United States.

BEFORE THE LECTURE

1 Building background knowledge on the topic

A The Montgomery Bus Boycott was one of the most important moments in the civil rights movement. During this protest, 17,000 African Americans refused to ride the segregated buses in Montgomery, Alabama. Read the passage below to learn more about the boycott.

> According to a law in 1955, African Americans in Montgomery had to sit at the back of city buses. They were also supposed to give up their seats to white passengers who were standing. Rosa Parks, who has been called "the mother of the freedom movement," was 42 years old at the time. On December 1, 1955, she was sitting at the back of the bus, as usual. When the white section filled up, the bus driver asked her to give up her seat. Parks refused to do so and was arrested. She also lost her job.
>
> Parks's act of civil disobedience resulted in a historic protest. Black residents of Montgomery circulated a flyer stating:
>
> *"Don't ride the buses to work, to town, to school, or anywhere on Monday. You can afford to stay out of school for one day if you have no other way to go except by bus. You can also afford to stay out of town for one day. If you work, take a cab or walk. But please, children and grown-ups, don't ride the bus at all on Monday. Please stay off all buses Monday."*
>
> The Montgomery Bus Boycott didn't last for just a day, however. It lasted for more than a year. Martin Luther King Jr. spent two weeks in jail because of his support for the boycott. Members of the African American community supported one another, walking, cycling, sharing car rides, and doing whatever they had to in order to get to their destination – except for riding the buses. In 1956, the Supreme Court declared that bus segregation was unconstitutional, and Martin Luther King rose to national importance as the leader of the civil rights movement.

B Work with a partner and answer the following questions.

1. What happened on December 1, 1955?

2. How did African Americans in Montgomery support the bus boycott?

3. How was Martin Luther King, Jr. involved in the boycott?

2 Listening for guiding questions Ⓛ Ⓝ

> Guiding questions are questions that speakers ask and answer themselves. These questions often introduce main ideas or important details. You should take notes on the questions and the answers. For example:
>
> The lecturer says:
> *First, I'm going to talk about the civil rights movement. Do you know about this period in U.S. history? The civil rights movement was the struggle by hundreds of thousands of people working over many years to achieve equal rights for African Americans.*
>
> You write:
> Civ rights movt =
> Strug. by 100,000s of people to achieve eq rts. for Af. Ams

A In the left column below, you will see the guiding questions that the lecturer asks. Read the questions and match them with answers from the column on the right.

Guiding questions

_____ 1. So, these are just a few examples of important events in the early struggle for civil rights. What happened next?

_____ 2. Today we can look back and be thankful for the great achievements of the civil rights movement. What were some of these achievements?

_____ 3. A journalist named Betty Friedan wrote a book called *The Feminine Mystique*. It was based on interviews with white, middle-class women living in the suburbs. And what do you think Friedan discovered?

_____ 4. Was the women's movement successful?

Answers

a. Well, first, the Jim Crow laws were overturned.

b. Well, these events led to more protests, more demonstrations, and more sit-ins throughout the '60s.

c. In some ways yes, of course. Today "equal pay for equal work" is the law.

d. She found that these women were very unhappy with their lives because of their lack of freedom and lack of a sense of identity.

B Now watch or listen to the questions and answers and check to see if you matched them correctly.

1 Guessing vocabulary from context Ⓥ

A The following items contain important vocabulary from Part 1 of the lecture. Work with a partner. Using the context and your knowledge of related words, take turns guessing the meanings of the words in **bold**.

_____ **1.** [At that time] there were many political and social **movements**.

_____ **2.** [These movements] **involved** thousands of people all over the nation.

_____ **3.** [These movements] **led to** new laws.

_____ **4.** [The civil rights movement was] the struggle by hundreds of thousands of people . . . to **achieve** equal rights for African Americans.

_____ **5.** . . . there were several **key** historical events.

_____ **6.** . . . the Jim Crow laws were **overturned**.

B Work with your partner. Match the vocabulary terms in Step A with their definitions below. Write the letters in the blanks next to the sentence or phrase containing the correct term in Step A. Check your answers in a dictionary if necessary.

a. caused (something) to happen

b. extremely important

c. get, gain

d. groups of people with the same ideas working together for a goal

e. made illegal

f. included

2 Creating your own symbols and abbreviations Ⓝ Ⓛ

In Chapter 2, you learned some common symbols and abbreviations to use in note taking. You should get in the habit of developing and using your own system of symbols and abbreviations. The system works best if you are able to automatically write and recognize your abbreviations.

A Work with a partner. Read the following list of key words and expressions from the lecture and create your own symbols or abbreviations for them.

Key word or expression	Symbol or abbreviation	Key word or expression	Symbol or abbreviation
1. African Americans		9. movement	
2. black		10. opportunities	
3. civil rights movement		11. rights	
4. demonstration		12. segregation	
5. education		13. students	
6. equal / equality		14. thousands	
7. inequality		15. women	
8. Martin Luther King Jr.		16. women's movement	

B Read the incomplete notes from Part 1 of Professor Smith's lecture on the civil rights movement. Notice that the note taker used columns to record the guiding questions and matching answers. Predict the kind of information you need to listen for to complete the notes.

Pt. 1: The _____

What was it?	strug. by _____ of people to achieve
	_____ for _____
How did it start?	100 yrs. after end of slav., _____ still common
	beg. of _____
Key events:	1. Dec 1, 1955: Rosa Parks _____
	_____ Montgomery bus _____
	2. 1960: blk. sts refused _____
	_____ = _____
	3. March 1963: march on _____
	_____ people heard _____
	give "I have a dream" speech.
_____?	More _____
	_____
_____?	1. Jim Crow laws overturned
	2. fed. gov't passed laws _____
	3. _____

C Now watch or listen to Part 1 of the lecture and complete the notes. Include your symbols and abbreviations from Step A.

D Work with a partner and compare notes. Then use them to review the guiding questions and matching answers.

1 Guessing vocabulary from context Ⓥ

A The following conversation contains important vocabulary from Part 2 of the lecture. Work with a partner. Using the context and your knowledge of related words, take turns guessing the meanings of the words in **bold**.

Guy: Hey, Ana – I was just reading a new (1) **best seller** about the history of the Women's Movement. Did you know that women played an important role during the Second World War?

Ana: Yes, of course I know that. That's when women (2) **took over** the jobs of thousands of men who were fighting abroad.

Guy: I didn't realize that before. Apparently, they built ships and worked in weapons factories, and hundreds of thousands served in the military.

Ana: That's why during the 1950s, women became so (3) **dissatisfied** with the traditional roles they had to go back to. They had almost no chance to become managers or (4) **executives**. Do you know about *The Feminine Mystique*?

Guy: Yes, I've read that book. It was based on interviews with white, middle-class women living in the (5) **suburbs**.

Ana: That's right. A lot of women at that time were very unhappy with their lives and with their (6) **lack** of freedom. They were expected to be full-time housewives, taking care of their husbands and the children.

Guy: Things have really changed since then, haven't they?

B Work with your partner. Match the vocabulary terms from Step A with their definitions below. Write the number on the line. Check your answers in a dictionary if necessary.

_____ **a.** the condition of not having something

_____ **b.** took another person's job or responsibilities

_____ **c.** high-level workers with the power to make decisions

_____ **d.** a book that sells a large number of copies

_____ **e.** residential areas outside an urban city

_____ **f.** not happy, not comfortable

2 Organizing your notes in a chart Ⓝ Ⓛ

> Organizing your notes in a chart allows you to see the main ideas and supporting details of a lecture clearly. Charts are also useful for taking notes on comparisons.

A Work with a partner. Study the following chart with notes from Part 2 of the lecture. Discuss: How did the speaker organize the lecture? What information is missing from the notes? What do you think the abbreviations mean?

Pt 2: The _____

WWII	1950s	1960s	Today
♂ fighting in Europe, Asia	→ ♀ started to feel dissat. w/ roles	1963: _____	Successes of WM:
♀: _____	– _____worked	Book showed _____	But _____
1945: _____	– earned _____ of what ♂ earned for = job	→ beg. of _____	Ineq. still exists
	– could be _____	Mid-60s: _____	
	– no ♀		

🔊 **B** Now watch or listen to Part 2 of the lecture and complete the notes. Use symbols
👥 and abbreviations.

C Work with a partner and compare your notes. Use them to retell the main events in the women's movement, decade by decade.

Reviewing your notes after a lecture ⓢ

> Review your notes soon after a lecture in order to fill in information that you missed and to check that your notes are clear and correct. It is a good idea to work with a partner and ask each other questions. For example: *What were the speaker's main points? What supporting details were provided? What did you learn?* Finally, you should copy your notes neatly using any of the formats you have learned in this book.

A Work in two groups. Group A will prepare review questions on the civil rights movement, and Group B will prepare questions on the women's movement.

Examples:

Group A: *What was the civil rights movement?*

Group B: *What did women do during World War II?*

Group A: The civil rights movement	Group B: The women's movement
1. _____ _____	1. _____ _____
2. _____ _____	2. _____ _____
3. _____ _____	3. _____ _____
4. _____ _____	4. _____ _____
5. _____ _____	5. _____ _____
6. _____ _____	6. _____ _____
7. _____ _____	7. _____ _____

B Now work in small groups that each include people from Group A and Group B. Take turns asking and answering each other's questions about the lecture.

Chapter 6
The Struggle Continues

Look at the photograph and answer the questions with your classmates.

1. Why do people stage protests and demonstrations? Why do you think the people in this photo are staging a demonstration?

2. Which groups of people are trying to achieve equality in the United States today?

1 Getting Started

In this section, you will read about progress toward equality in the United States since the 1960s. You will also hear people talk about experiences in which they felt they received unfair treatment.

1 Reading and thinking about the topic ⓥ ⓢ

A Read the following passage.

In the 1960s, important laws were passed to protect the rights of African Americans and women. The passage of these laws encouraged other groups, such as Hispanics (also known as Latinos),* older people (senior citizens), Native Americans, and people with disabilities to struggle for greater equality.

These groups have achieved some success in their struggles. For example, Latino protests led to the introduction of ethnic studies programs at colleges across the country. New laws guarantee that older Americans have more access to public services, like transportation. And now, by law, public schools must provide assistance for children with disabilities.

However, the struggle for equality in the United States is not finished. Although laws have been passed to protect the rights of many groups, the laws are not always enforced. Furthermore, laws cannot change people's attitudes. Despite the laws, *racism* (prejudice against people of different racial groups), *sexism* (prejudice against men or women because of their sex), *ageism* (prejudice against people because of their age), and prejudice against people with disabilities still exist. The struggle for equality includes trying to eliminate *stereotypes* (unfair, inaccurate generalizations) and promoting *tolerance* (acceptance) for all groups.

B Answer the following questions according to the information in the passage.

1. What are some groups that have struggled for equality since the 1960s?
2. What were some of the achievements of these groups?
3. Why is it necessary to continue the struggle for equality today?

C Read these questions and share your responses with a partner.

1. What are some examples of stereotypes? Why are stereotypes unfair?
2. What are some examples of inequality that you know about in other countries?

The terms Hispanic *and* Latino *are both commonly used.*

2 Listening for specific information Ⓛ Ⓝ Ⓢ

A You will hear four people describe situations in which they believe they were treated unfairly. Read the summaries below before listening and predict the type of information you need to listen for.

1. Peter is _____ years old. _____ months ago, he lost his job as a _____ because the company didn't have _____ for him. But then the company hired a new _____ who is _____ years old.

2. Theresa is a _____ . Last week she had an _____ for a job with a _____ . It went well until _____ when the interviewer asked her if she was pregnant. She said _____ . She didn't get the job.

3. Robert is married and has _____ children. Last week, he and his wife filled out an application for a new _____ . However, they didn't get it. A friend told them it's because nobody else in the building has _____ and the manager is worried about _____ .

4. Rebecca is a _____ who uses a _____ . One of her classes is on the _____ floor, and the building has only two _____ , so she has been _____ to class a few times. She explained the problem to her professor, but he said he expects her to come to class _____ just like everyone else.

B Now listen to the four people and fill in the blanks in Step A.

C Compare answers in small groups. Then, for each situation, discuss the following questions: Do you believe the speaker was treated fairly or unfairly? Why or why not?

2 Real-Life Voices

In this section, you will hear an interview with Robin, who works with the blind. Then you will hear Jairo and Sandy discuss progress toward equality for two groups that regularly face discrimination.

BEFORE THE INTERVIEWS

1 Thinking critically about the topic Ⓢ

A Read these blogs and take notes on the writers' opinions.

Blog 1

I recently saw the movie *Battle in the Hood*, and I was shocked by its message about African Americans. The movie suggests that we are all poor and violent. That is such a negative stereotype! Isn't it about time that movies portray African Americans as hardworking, law-abiding citizens? Why don't they make more films showing minority groups in a more positive way?

Blog 2

I am writing to express my anger about employers who harass workers for speaking Spanish while they are at work. I support the language rights of all immigrant communities in the United States whose first language is not English. People should be able to speak their own language to their co-workers, as long as they are doing their jobs.

Blog 3

As a person with a physical disability, I am pleased the government is at last paying attention to the needs of the disabled. However, I have to tell you that many public places are still hard to get around. For example, I usually can't use public transportation because the elevators are often not available or are out of service.

Blog 4

Yesterday I was out shopping with a group of friends, and we were surprised to find a sign that said only two of us could enter a store at one time. I didn't know they allowed things like that. Why do older people always treat us with suspicion, like we are going to steal something or cause trouble?

B Work with a partner and share your responses.

1. Which group does each blog describe?
2. What problem is each writer describing?
3. Why are the writers upset?

2 Building background knowledge on the topic

A How much do you know about the following groups of people? Work with a partner. Read the facts below, and guess the correct answer.

Disabled individuals

1. Percentage of disabled adults who are unemployed
   a. 4%   **b.** 21%   **c.** 59%
2. Percentage of adults with severe disabilities who live in poverty
   a. 9%   **b.** 11%   **c.** 28%

Hispanics

3. Percentage of Hispanics who complete four years of college
   a. 13%   **b.** 25%   **c.** 46%
4. Which is the largest Hispanic population in the United States?
   a. Mexicans   **b.** Dominicans   **c.** Cubans

Senior citizens

5. Percentage of the U.S. population over age 65
   a. 6%   **b.** 13%   **c.** 22%
6. Average life expectancy in the United States
   a. 69   **b.** 78   **c.** 82

B With your partner, look at the correct answers at the bottom of this page. Then discuss your responses. What did you learn that will help you understand these groups better?

1 Examining vocabulary in context

Here are some words and phrases from the interviews printed in **bold** and given in the context in which you will hear them. They are followed by definitions.

[Latinos] are the largest **minority group** in the United States: *a group of people from a particular racial, ethnic, or religious background other than the white majority*

[Latinos] have made significant **contributions** to American society: *something people do or give in order to make something better or more successful*

Hospitals should have **interpreters**: *people who translate from one language to another*

. . . patients don't have to struggle to explain their **symptoms** in English: *evidence of medical problems*

There's still a lot of **poverty** in the Hispanic community: *the condition of being poor*

There are laws, but they're really hard to **enforce**: *make people obey*

A lot of times, bosses think there's a **risk** to hiring older people: *danger*

. . . if he's got two **applicants** for a job: *people trying to get a job*

2 Listening for main ideas

A Look at the chart below and notice the information you need to listen for in the interview.

	Group	Progress toward equality	Problems that still exist
Jairo			
Sandy			
Me			

B Now listen to the interview and fill in the first two rows of your chart with the information you hear.

C Work with a partner and compare answers. Then choose a group in the United States or another country that you would like to discuss. Write notes on the group you choose in the third row of the chart above. Discuss your ideas with a partner.

1 Examining vocabulary in context ⓥ

Here are some words and phrases from the interview with Robin, printed in **bold** and given in the context in which you will hear them. They are followed by definitions.

There are computers that can "talk," and software that prints documents in **Braille**: *a system of printing that allows blind people to read by touching with their fingers*

There are many simple **gadgets** . . . that can help: *small machines*

. . . a tray . . . is one of the simplest **aids**: *things that help*

By folding a **bill** a certain way . . . : *paper money, such as $5 or $10*

You leave **singles** flat: *one-dollar bills ($1)*

. . . after that, you can learn to take care of things **on your own**: *without help from others*

Imagine people feeling that their problems are **overwhelming**: *too big to manage or control*

2 Listening for specific information Ⓛ Ⓢ

A Robin works with blind people. In the interview, she talks about ways that blind people can live and work more independently. Look at the pictures below and discuss this question with a partner: How do you think the items in the pictures can help blind people?

It's nine o'clock

a. _____   b. _____   c. _____

d. _____   e. _____

B Now listen to the interview. Write the names of the items in the blanks in Step A.

C Work with a partner and compare your answers. Discuss how these items make life easier for the blind.

3 Listening for tone of voice 🅛 🅢

🔊 **A** Listen again to excerpts from the interview with Robin. Circle the adjective that best describes Robin's tone of voice.

Excerpt One

Robin is discussing the work that blind people do in offices.

She sounds _____ .

    a. optimistic   **b.** unhappy   **c.** surprised

Excerpt Two

Robin is discussing everyday activities that blind people have to do, just like everyone else.

She sounds _____ .

    a. serious   **b.** impatient   **c.** angry

Excerpt Three

Robin is explaining what is involved in her job.

She sounds _____ .

    a. confused   **b.** enthusiastic   **c.** upset

B Compare your answers with a partner.

AFTER THE INTERVIEWS

Sharing your opinion 🅢

Mix It Up is a national campaign in schools that fights prejudice and promotes tolerance for others. One activity involves students sitting at different tables during lunchtime. That way, they can meet other students they don't usually associate with.

A Mark each statement *A* (agree) or *D* (disagree). Then explain your responses to the class.

_____ Most people develop opinions about others, even before they speak to them.

_____ People usually make friends only with others who are similar to themselves.

_____ It is hard to accept other people if they have different beliefs or values from yours.

_____ It is painful to be rejected by others.

_____ If school children learn about tolerance, they will be more accepting of others.

_____ Sitting with different groups, at school or college, can help to promote tolerance.

B Read the poem "Walls: A Poem for Tolerance" in the left column below. It is by Pebbles Salas, a student in the eighth grade. With a partner, answer the questions in the right column.

Walls:
A Poem for Tolerance

People make boundaries
they classify who's who.
Even if they don't know you,
they classify you too.
Whether it's color or style,
they'll file you down
to which groups you can be with,
and which groups you can't hang around.
People don't see the good and the bad,
they just imagine your face,
would it look good on an ad?
People are sad when they get rejected
they sit with a different group
to feel protected.
But social boundaries can be such a drag,
you wrap up new friendships in one little bag.
Would you want one pair of friends,
or would you care for two?
That decision is solely up to you.
So if you sit at the same table every day,
there will be no new friendships,
only old friendships will stay.

1. What do most people do, in Pebbles's opinion? What consequence does this have?

2. What do people imagine, according to Pebbles? Why is this bad, in her opinion?
3. How do people feel when they are not accepted? What do they do, and why?
4. What are social boundaries? What does Pebbles think of them?

5. What should people do if they want to have more friends?

boundaries: *limits*
file you down: *limit you*
hang around: *be with*
ad: *advertisement*
get rejected: *are not accepted*
such a drag: *really bad*
wrap up: *put*
solely: *only*

C Work in small groups and discuss the following questions.

1. What is the meaning of the word *Walls* in the title of the poem?
2. What is the main point that Pebbles is making?
3. How might this poem be different if it were about adults or people in their late teens?
4. If Jairo and Sandy read this poem, what do you think they would say?
5. Do you think poetry can be helpful in making people aware of the importance of being tolerant?

D Look at the photograph below. How does it illustrate the ideas in "Walls"?

3 In Your Own Voice

In this section, you will participate in an activity that explores stereotypes, tolerance, and discrimination. Then you will give a group presentation about what you learned.

Thinking critically about the topic ⓢ

> You will not always agree with what you read or hear. Make it a habit to evaluate what other people say and compare it to your own knowledge and experiences.

A Work in small groups. Read the descriptions of the four activities below and choose one that your group would like to do.

Activity 1: Examine gender roles

Make a two-column chart, one column headed "Men" and the other column headed "Women." Then choose a general-interest magazine and count the number of men and women in the advertisements. Put this information next to the headings in the appropriate column. Underneath, list the roles that the men and women are playing, for example, husband, wife, teacher, athlete, businessperson, and so on. Analyze the results of your research. Are there more women or more men in the ads? What roles do they play? Are these stereotypical roles, or do they show men and women in a realistic way?

Activity 2: Discuss a poster

Work with a partner and look at the poster below. First, decide what message it is communicating, and then come up with a title for the poster. Share your idea with the class and vote on the best title.

Activity 3: Analyze quotes about tolerance

Choose two or three of the quotations below or find others by doing an Internet search for "tolerance quotations" or "quotations about tolerance." Discuss the meaning of the quotations and give examples from your experience that show why you agree or disagree with them.

"You must look into people, as well as at them."

Lord Chesterfield (1694–1773), British statesman

"Sometimes I feel discriminated against, but it does not make me angry. It merely astonishes me. How can any deny themselves the pleasure of my company?"

Zora Neale Hurston (1891–1960), American novelist

"People are very open-minded about new things – as long as they're exactly like the old ones."

Charles F. Kettering (1876–1958), American inventor

"Darkness cannot drive out darkness; only light can do that. Hate cannot drive out hate; only love can do that."

Dr. Martin Luther King Jr. (1929–1968), American civil rights leader

"The only way to make sure people you agree with can speak is to support the rights of people you don't agree with."

Eleanor Holmes Norton (1937–), member of U.S. House of Representatives

"Those wearing tolerance for a label call other views intolerable."

Phyllis McGinley (1905–1978), American poet

Activity 4: Share an experience of discrimination

Tell the members of your group about a time when someone discriminated against you because of your race, religion, academic ability, athletic ability, hobbies, interests, gender, personal appearance, family income, home environment, or other factor. Explain how you felt and why you think you were the victim of discrimination. Listen to your classmates' stories. Discuss the similarities and differences between their experiences and yours.

B When you have finished your activity, discuss the following questions with the members of your group.

1. What did you learn from doing this activity?

2. What was the most interesting part of the activity?

4 Academic Listening and Note Taking

In this section, you will hear and take notes on a two-part lecture given by David Chachere, a lecturer on political science. The title of his lecture is "Two Important Laws in the Struggle for Equality."

BEFORE THE LECTURE

1 Sharing your opinion ⓢ

Look at the photographs below and discuss the following questions with a partner:

1. What do the people in the photographs have in common?
2. What difficulties do these people probably face?
3. How could laws help these people to participate fully in society?

Student

Woodworker

Office worker

Athlete

2 Listening for signal words and phrases

Good lecturers use *signal words and phrases* to help listeners follow the organization of their lectures and to understand the relationship between ideas. Signal words and phrases have many different purposes. For example:

Purpose	Signal words and phrases
To add an idea	*also / as well as / in addition*
To emphasize	*of course / in fact*
To indicate difference	*however / in contrast / on the other hand*
To indicate similarity	*(just) like / similar to*
To indicate time	*before / after / while / during*
To introduce a cause or reason	*because / since*
To introduce an effect	*as a result / therefore / consequently*
To introduce a topic or change the topic	*as for / speaking of / in terms of*
To list information or ideas	*first / second / next / last / to begin*
To refer to information mentioned earlier	*to refresh your memory / remember / as I said*
To repeat an idea with different words	*in other words / that is*
To show order of importance	*more / the most important*
To signal an incomplete list	*et cetera / and so forth / and so on*

A Work with a partner. Read the following sentences from the lecture and try to predict which signal words or phrases from the box go in the blanks.

1. _____ . . . the '60s was an important decade because during this time several important laws gave more rights to women, African Americans, and immigrants.

2. Let's begin with the first one, the Age Discrimination Act. I think we need to talk about, _____ , the reasons why this law was needed; second, what it does; and _____ , its impact.

3. _____ this law, employers could set an age limit for job applicants.

4. Well, of course, it [the law] refers to hiring and firing. _____ , age can't be used as a reason for refusing to hire an older person.

5. _____ , age can't be used as a reason to promote someone to a better position.

6. The ADA _____ covers people who face discrimination _____ they have a serious illness like cancer.

7. _____ mental disabilities, there has been progress, too.

8. But I think _____ impact of this law is that it's helped to change the way we think.

9. In many places in the world, people with disabilities have to stay at home _____ there is no way for them to get around.

B Watch or listen and fill in the blanks with the signal words or phrases you hear.

C Work with your partner and compare answers. Then select other signal words and phrases from the box that are appropriate for the blanks.

1 Guessing vocabulary from context Ⓥ

A The following presentation contains important vocabulary from Part 1 of the lecture. Work with a partner. Using the context and your knowledge of related words, take turns trying to guess the meanings of the words in **bold**.

Manager:

Good morning, everybody. Well, let me say, on behalf of the company, that we are very pleased that you have sent in an application letter. Today, I'm going to be giving you a short orientation to the company, including a description of (1) **benefits** our employees receive. We understand that you are much more (2) **likely** to do well here if you understand company policy.

Let's begin by thinking of the company as a place to build your career. We think it is important to recognize the efforts of our employees, and we usually (3) **promote** people who do well. Some of our employees have been with us for decades, and there is no age when we make you stop working. That's against the law, and in any case, we believe that a company should not force anyone to (4) **retire**. As far as we're concerned, retirement is a personal choice.

Now let's talk about holidays and sick days. Well, the board of directors recently (5) **set** some new guidelines. There are nine paid holidays, five days of vacation, and five days of sick leave. If you wish to use sick leave for your own purposes, that is fine with us. It's not (6) **mandatory** to bring a doctor's note unless you are out for more than three days in a row.

You probably think that these benefits sound very attractive. Well, we do, too. And let me tell you, our policies have had a huge (7) **impact** on our employees. We receive very few (8) **complaints**. And why should we? This company is a great place to work. So we look forward to having a personal interview with you all. Maybe this is the kind of company you are looking for. If so, we would like to meet with you in an interview.

B Work with your partner. Match the vocabulary terms from Step A with their definitions below. Write the number on the line. Check your answers in a dictionary if necessary.

_____ **a.** stop working because of your age

_____ **b.** effect, result

_____ **c.** move a person up to a higher level in a job

_____ **d.** made, established

_____ **e.** required, forced, done because you must

_____ **f.** advantages people get from their employers besides their salaries, such as health insurance

_____ **g.** statements that people say when something is wrong or not satisfactory

_____ **h.** probable

2 Indenting Ⓝ

Indenting can help you to see the difference between main ideas and supporting details. You can use indenting with other note-taking techniques, such as bullets, numbers, or letters. Continue to indent as the information becomes more specific.

For example:
I. First main idea (not indented)
    1. First supporting idea (indented 5 spaces from the left margin)
        • **Example or detail** (indented 10 spaces)
    2. Second supporting idea (indented 5 spaces)
        • **Example or detail** (indented 10 spaces)

A Below are a student's notes on Part 1 of the lecture. But it is hard to follow them because the student didn't separate main ideas from supporting ideas or examples. Read the notes and try to predict which items are main ideas and which ones are supporting ideas or examples.

Age Discrim. in Employment Act
Why law was needed
Older people faced discrim. in wkplace
Before law, employers could set age limits, ex. 35

What the law does
Protects people > 40 from discrim.
Can't use age to
refuse to hire
fire
promote to a better position

Impact of law
Nowadays, nothing about age in job app
Equal benefits for older + younger people
No mandatory retirement

Do employers follow law?
1,000s of complaints per year > age discrim. still exists.
Recent study showed companies 40% more likely to
interview younger applicant.
But: People are more aware of age discrim. than before law

B Now watch or listen to Part 1 of the lecture. Mark the main ideas, supporting ideas, and examples by writing numbers, bullets, or other symbols you prefer in the left margin.

C Rewrite the notes on your own paper with the symbols you chose in Step B. Be sure to indent appropriately.

D Work in small groups and compare your notes. Use them to retell the information in Part 1 of the lecture.

1 Guessing vocabulary from context Ⓥ

A The following items contain important vocabulary from Part 2 of the lecture. Work with a partner. Using the context and your knowledge of related words, take turns guessing the meanings of the words in **bold**.

_____ **1.** . . . the Americans with Disabilities Act, which is often called the ADA **for short**.

_____ **2.** By "disability" we mean . . . any physical or **mental condition** that limits a person's ability to participate in a major life activity . . .

_____ **3.** If you've ridden a public bus in an American city, . . . you know that they all have special **mechanisms** . . .

_____ **4.** In many places in the world, . . . there is no way for [people with disabilities] to **get around**.

_____ **5.** . . . they are also often **rejected** by society.

_____ **6.** Let the **shameful** wall of exclusion finally come tumbling down.

_____ **7.** What this means is that our goal needs to be **inclusion**.

B Work with your partner. Match the vocabulary terms in Step A with their definitions below. Write the letters in the blanks next to the sentence or phrase containing the correct term in Step A. Check your answers in a dictionary if necessary.

a. causing great embarrassment

b. technology, gadgets

c. a sickness of the mind that affects people's behavior and emotions

d. as an abbreviation

e. move from place to place

f. the act of including everybody, accepting everybody

g. unwanted, not accepted

2 Using an outline Ⓝ

Using an outline is a useful way to organize notes. In a formal outline, main ideas are usually listed using Roman numerals (I, II, III, etc.). Subdivisions of main ideas are indicated as capital letters (A, B, C, etc.). Supporting details are listed using Arabic numerals (1, 2, 3, etc.). Each level of detail is indented under the level above it.

You may not be able to organize your notes carefully while you are actually listening to a lecture. In that case, you should rewrite your notes as soon as possible after the lecture and put them into an appropriate, well-organized outline.

A Look at the outlined notes for the beginning of Part 2 of the lecture below. Work with a partner and discuss the following questions.

1. What is the main idea of this section of Part 2?
2. What are the subdivisions of the main idea?
3. Which examples are given?

The Americans with Disabilities Act (ADA)

I. ADA
    A. Passed in 1990
    B. Protects ppl w/ disabil. in diff places, ex:
        1. work
        2. housing
        3. educ.

B Look at a student's notes for the rest of the lecture. They are not in outline form. Read the notes and try to predict which items are main ideas, which ones are subdivisions of main ideas, and which ones are supporting details.

Def. of "disability":
Physical
Mental

Impact of ADA
Changed life for disabled people, ex.
Buses have mechanisms to help ppl in wheelchairs
doorways must be wide
some businesses hiring ppl w/ nonphysical (mental) disab
Sts w/ learning disab can get more time on tests

Most important impact of law: Change ppl's thinking
Some countries: Disabled stay home b/c no way to get around
U.S. Understand there are many things disabled ppl can do
Pres. Bush (1990): "Let the shameful wall of exclusion finally come tumbling down."
Goal must be inclusion

C Now watch or listen to Part 2 of the lecture. Put the notes above into an outline by writing roman numerals, capital letters, and numbers in appropriate places in the left margin.

D Rewrite the notes in outline form on your own paper.

E Work in small groups and compare your notes. Use them to retell the information in Part 2 of the lecture.

Using your notes to make a time line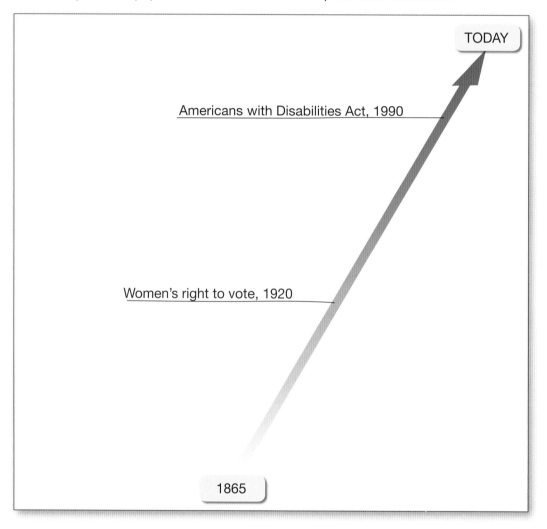

When you are studying a topic in which events and their dates are important, it is useful to make a time line from the information in your notes. This helps you review what you have learned in a visual way.

A Work with a partner. Use the information from Chapters 5 and 6 to construct a time line of important steps the United States has taken toward equality. You can either make a time line on your own paper or add lines to the incomplete time line below.

TODAY

Americans with Disabilities Act, 1990

Women's right to vote, 1920

1865

B As you work, discuss the following question: What are the causes and the effects of each event in your time line?

C As a class, compare the information in your time lines. Make a class time line on the board.

Unit 3 Academic Vocabulary Review

This section reviews the vocabulary from Chapters 5 and 6. For a complete list all of the Academic Word List words in this book, see the Appendix on page 182.

A Complete the exercises below.

I. Match the words on the left with their definition on the right.

_____ **1.** aware   **a.** merit, advantage

_____ **2.** segregation   **b.** a strike or protest

_____ **3.** boycott   **c.** separation

_____ **4.** significant   **d.** conscious, familiar

_____ **5.** benefit   **e.** remarkable, important

II. Use a word from the box to fill in the blanks. Use the correct form of the word.

goal   impact   positive   promote

Professional development, which is a way to improve workers' skills and knowledge, has an important (1) _____ : that is, it is trying to give everyone in a company the chance to keep improving their performance. Most employees want to reach their full potential. Good employers encourage them by (2) _____ workers who do well.

Obviously, some development programs are better than others. Some of the programs that companies offer are seen as a waste of time. Others, however, can have a big (3) _____ on job performance. The most important factor in these programs is how well the group leader connects with the employees. Trainers who are optimistic and (4) _____ tend to get better results.

III. Use the correct form of the words in the box to complete the sentences.

achievement, achieve   reaction, react
creation, creativity, create   tradition(s), traditional, traditionally
discrimination, discriminate

1. _____ against children who are different from others is a big problem in schools across the country.

2. That is why many schools have begun to _____ special programs to teach children tolerance.

3. These programs are trying to teach children to respect each other's _____ and customs.

4. Many parents believe that if we can promote tolerance among young people, it will be a great _____

5. Children who have been involved in Mix it Up, a national campaign to promote greater interaction, have had a very positive _____ .

B Use the academic vocabulary from Step A to answer the following questions in pairs or as a class.

Before the 1960s

1. What were the Fourteenth and the Nineteenth Amendments?
2. What were the Jim Crow laws, and what was segregation?
3. What were the main jobs women had before the 1960s?

The Civil Rights Movement and the Women's Movement

4. What happened during the 1960s?
5. What progress did African Americans make during this time?
6. What was *The Feminine Mystique*, and why was it so important?

Issues of Equality

7. What makes it easier for disabled people to participate more fully in society?
8. What problems do Hispanics often confront in American society?
9. Why does age affect people's opportunities?

Important Laws

10. What is the Americans with Disabilities Act (ADA)?
11. When did age discrimination in employment become illegal?
12. Have the Age Discrimination in Employment Act and the ADA been successful?

Oral Presentation

In groups, you will research an individual who represents the struggle for equality in the United States. Then you will make a poster about this person and present it to the class.

BEFORE THE PRESENTATION

A Work with a small group of two to three people. Choose a person to research from the list below.

Susan B. Anthony	Abraham Lincoln	Rosa Parks
George Washington Carver	Martin Luther King Jr.	Paul Robeson
César Chávez	Lucretia Mott	Sonia Sotomayor
Frederick Douglass	Barack Obama	Elizabeth Cady Stanton
Betty Friedan	Jackie Robinson	Other (your own choice)

B Make a poster that illustrates what you find (an example appears below). Include photos or pictures and details about the person's:

- date and place of birth and/or death
- achievements and struggle for equality
- most important contributions to society
- other interesting information

Dates and Details About George Washington Carver

He was born into slavery around 1864 (exact date unknown).

After slavery was abolished, his former master, Moses Carver, raised him as his own child.

He died in 1943.

Profession
Scientist (botanist), educator, and inventor

Education and Achievements:
As a young child, Carver had to move 10 miles from his home to attend a school that admitted black children. When he was older, he was rejected from college because of his race. However, he was eventually accepted at another college, became the first black student there, and after he graduated, became the first black professor at the college. Later on in life, as a professional, Carver achieved national recognition for his work.

Significance
Carver was inspired by this advice from a woman who helped him go to school:

"You must learn all you can, then go back out into the world and give your learning back to the people."

He believed passionately in social harmony, although he saw a lot of injustice in his life, including the effects of segregation and extreme violence against blacks.

As a scientist and educator, Carver used his skills to improve the quality of life of poor black farmers in the South. He promoted the cultivation of peanuts and sweet potatoes instead of cotton. His work in crop rotation led to important progress in agriculture and nutrition for millions of people, black and white.

On his grave, it says:

"He could have added fortune to fame, but caring for neither, he found happiness and honor in being helpful to the world."

C As a group, prepare a short presentation on the person you have researched. Decide which students in your group will present which parts of the information you found. Practice your presentation aloud at least once.

DURING THE PRESENTATION

A Put your posters on the wall. As a class, take turns looking at other groups' posters and listening to their presentations. When the other students look at your poster, explain it to them. Use the poster as a guide, but add other information you have learned.

B As you look at the posters:

- ask the speakers to explain something you did not understand
  Example: *Can you talk some more about the injustice George Washington Carver saw?*
- ask for more information about what you see and hear
  Example: *Could you tell me about the national recognition George Washington Carver achieved?*
- make a comment on what you see and hear
  Example: *I like the quotations you chose. I learned how Carver spent his life helping other people.*

C While showing your poster, take turns answering your classmates' questions and responding to their comments.

AFTER THE PRESENTATION

A In your group, perform a self-assessment. Ask yourself the following questions.

Did you . . .

- [ ] learn interesting information about progress toward equality?
- [ ] work well with other class members to make and explain your poster?
- [ ] present the information you learned in an interesting and accessible way?
- [ ] take turns explaining the information to other groups?
- [ ] respond to the questions and comments that other students made?
- [ ] ask questions and make comments about the other posters?

B As a class, make a master list of the information you have learned. Discuss the most interesting facts that were presented.

Unit 4
American Values

Independence Day
celebration

In this unit, you will consider some of the values that defined the United States
in the past and that still play an important role in people's lives today. Chapter
7 focuses on some of the traditional values that form the foundation of American
culture and society. You will hear interviews with people about values that
are important to them. The lecture in this chapter focuses on three American
folk heroes and the values they represent. Chapter 8 concerns ways in which
traditional values have changed in modern America. You will hear young people
talking about differences between their values and those of their parents. You
will also hear a teacher talking about values that are important for students to
learn. The lecture is about conservative and liberal political views in America.

Contents

In Unit 4, you will listen to and speak about the following topics.

Chapter 7 American Values from the Past	Chapter 8 American Values Today
Interview 1 Personal Values **Interview 2** Values in Theory and in Practice **Lecture** Three American Folk Heroes	**Interview 1** Differences in Values Between Parents and Children **Interview 2** Values in the Workplace **Lecture** Conservative and Liberal Values in American Politics

Skills

In Unit 4, you will practice the following skills.

L Listening Skills	**S** Speaking Skills
Listening for specific information Listening for tone of voice Listening for main ideas Listening for key words Listening for stressed words Listening for general statements	Sharing your opinion Answering true/false questions Sharing your knowledge Drawing inferences Role-playing Conducting a survey
V Vocabulary Skills	**N** Note Taking Skills
Reading and thinking about the topic Building background knowledge on the topic Examining vocabulary in context Guessing vocabulary from context	Clarifying your notes Taking notes on questions and answers Taking notes in a point-by-point format Using information on the board to help you take notes

Learning Outcomes

Prepare and **deliver** an oral presentation on a value you consider important

Chapter 7
American Values from the Past

Look at the photograph and answer the questions with a partner.

1. What does this photograph show? What are the people in the photo doing?

2. What values does this photograph communicate?

1 Getting Started

In this section, you will learn about some traditional values that many Americans hold.

1 Reading and thinking about the topic

A Read the following passage.

Values are beliefs that help us decide what is right and wrong and how we should behave in various situations. Values guide our personal, social, and business behavior and affect every aspect of our daily lives.

Many Western values are based on beliefs that originally came from both the ancient Greek and Roman civilizations and the religious beliefs of Judaism and Christianity. American values are also based on these beliefs. However, the beliefs of the Protestant branch of Christianity have been particularly important in American culture. Many of America's early settlers and leaders came from a Protestant tradition that emphasizes hard work. Sometimes, therefore, the value of hard work is referred to as "the Protestant work ethic." Traditional American values include hard work, self-reliance, equality, freedom, individualism, justice, and democracy. All of these values have defined American culture since the earliest days of the nation's history.

B Answer the following questions according to the information in the passage.

1. What are values? What purpose do values serve?
2. Which cultures and religions have influenced American values?
3. What are some key American values?

C Read these questions and share your responses with a partner.

1. Do you think that most values are the same from culture to culture?
2. What are three or four values that you believe in?

2 Listening for specific information Ⓛ Ⓢ

A Read the following paragraph.

Horatio Alger was a famous nineteenth-century American author who wrote more than 130 novels for young readers. Many of these best-selling novels were about poor orphan boys who climbed the ladder of success. They achieved the "American Dream" through their hard work, honesty, and determination. Alger's books encouraged readers to believe in traditional American values. According to these beliefs, even the poor could achieve success and social recognition if they worked hard enough and had the proper moral values.

◀)) **B** Read this summary of a Horatio Alger story written in 1877. Then listen and underline the details you hear.

The title of this story is "Wait and Hope." It is about a boy called (1) (*Steve / Ben*), whose parents (2) (*have died / are very poor*). The boy (3) (*has a lot of friends who help him / has few friends*), but he refuses to lose hope. He feels very (4) (*sad / positive*) about his life. One day, he meets a (5) (*rich stranger / lost relative*), who gives him a job. He works hard at school and finally manages to begin studying at (6) (*Princeton University / Harvard University*). His story shows that if you have (7) (*patience and strength / good luck and determination*), you will eventually find success.

C Share your reactions to this story with your classmates. Discuss these questions.

1. Which values does this story illustrate?
2. Are these values important to you?
3. Why do you think this kind of story has always been so popular in America?

2 Real-Life Voices

In this section, you will hear three Americans talk about values that are important to them. You will also hear about values that sometimes create disagreement.

BEFORE THE INTERVIEWS

1 Building background knowledge on the topic Ⓥ

L. Robert Kohls was a writer and teacher in the field of intercultural studies. In a famous paper called "The Values Americans Live By," written in the 1980s, Dr. Kohls described 13 basic values that help explain American attitudes and behavior.

A Read Kohls's list of values below. Check (✓) five values that are very important to you and explain to a partner why they are important.

_____ action and work   _____ individualism

_____ change (change is good)   _____ informality

_____ competition   _____ materialism

_____ directness/honesty   _____ personal control and determination

_____ efficiency   _____ self-reliance

_____ equality   _____ value of time

_____ future orientation (the future is
better than the past)

B Proverbs are very old sayings. They show cultural values and ways of acting. Read the example below. It's a proverb that illustrates one of Kohls's values.

> **Proverb:** Never put off until tomorrow what you can do today.

Value that the proverb illustrates: a. ~~competition~~ b. ~~equality~~ c. action and work

Form two groups. Look at the chart with the proverbs and values. Each group should match a proverb or saying on the left with a value listed in the right column.
Write the letter of the value in the blank space.

GROUP A	
Proverbs and sayings	Values
_____ 1. The only thing that's constant is change. _____ 2. A stitch in time saves nine. _____ 3. Winning isn't everything; it's the only thing. _____ 4. All good things come to those who wait. _____ 5. Honesty is the best policy. _____ 6. Green leaves and brown leaves fall from the same tree.	a. change b. competition c. directness/honesty d. efficiency e. equality f. future orientation

GROUP B	
Proverbs and sayings	Values
_____ 1. Where there's a will there's a way. _____ 2. There are only 24 hours in a day. _____ 3. A penny saved is a penny earned. _____ 4. Don't be ashamed to blow your own horn. _____ 5. There's no need to stand on ceremony. _____ 6. God helps those who help themselves.	a. individualism b. informality c. materialism d. personal control and determination e. self-reliance f. the value of time

C When you are finished, share your group's answers with the other group.

D Discuss these questions.

1. From your experience, do you agree that the values listed above are important to Americans?

2. What are some other values that you think are important to Americans?

2 Sharing your opinion ⓢ

A Read the situations below and circle the letter, *a* or *b*, that comes closest to your reaction.

1. Your neighbor says: "My daughter's going to drop her physics class and take music instead. She says physics is too hard. I'm worried she won't be able to get into a top university."

    You think:

    a. I agree with the daughter. Why should she take a subject she's not interested in?

    b. The daughter should just work harder at physics. She needs to think about her future.

2. Your 20-year-old friend says: "I'm going to work at a bookstore and keep going to school full-time."

    You say:

    a. "That's a bad idea. Your grades will probably go down, and you'll be too tired to spend time with friends."

    b. "That's a good idea. You'll learn how to be responsible and manage your time better."

3. Your 45-year-old father says: "I've decided I don't really like my job. I want to go back to school and change careers."

    You say:

    a. "I don't think you should do that. You're too old to go back to school."

    b. "That's great. You've worked hard for 20 years, and now you deserve the chance to do a job you really enjoy."

4. Your professor comes to class wearing jeans.

    You think:

    a. I feel comfortable with a teacher who dresses informally.

    b. I can't respect a teacher who dresses like a student.

5. At the bank, the teller calls you by your first name.

    You think:

    a. That's disrespectful.

    b. I like the casual, friendly atmosphere of this bank.

B Work with a partner and compare your answers. Which values explain your point of view in each case?

1 Examining vocabulary in context **V**

Here are some words and phrases from the interview with Marielena and Dan, printed in **bold** and given in the context in which you will hear them. They are followed by definitions.

> . . . my parents have high **expectations** for the children in my family: *goals, hopes*
>
> I want her to realize that she has **options**: *possibilities, choices*
>
> I think there are many ways to be happy and **productive**: *useful, creative*
>
> I want my daughter to be good at something that is **meaningful**: *important or serious*
>
> The first [value] I think of is hard work. And **self-reliance**: *depending on yourself*
>
> . . . especially in this **economic climate**: *current economic situation*
>
> Having a job helps you to **set** goals and work toward them: *create, decide upon*

2 Answering true/false questions **S** **L**

> When answering true/false questions, you are sometimes given three options: *T* (true), *F* (false), or *NI* (not enough information). You should respond *NI* if the speaker does not provide enough details for you to decide if a statement is true or false.

A Read the following statements before you listen to the interview with Marielena and Dan.

Marielena

_____ **1.** The value that Marielena considers most important is education.

_____ **2.** Marielena has a daughter and a son.

_____ **3.** Her daughter is 15.

_____ **4.** There are many artists in Marielena's family.

_____ **5.** She thinks her daughter might become a painter or an actress.

_____ **6.** Marielena's friend wants to change careers.

Dan

_____ **1.** The value Dan considers most important is competition.

_____ **2.** Dan is 20 years old.

_____ **3.** He thinks it is important to improve yourself.

_____ **4.** Dan just started college.

_____ **5.** Dan wants to go to graduate school.

_____ **6.** His part-time job is in a restaurant.

B Now listen to the interviews. Write *T* (true), *F* (false), or *NI* (not enough information) next to each of the statements. Then work with a partner and compare your answers to Step A.

C List on a separate piece of paper the values that Marielena and Dan discuss. Do you agree with their opinions?

3 Listening for tone of voice Ⓛ Ⓢ

A Read the excerpts and sentence stems. Predict which phrase you think will correctly complete the stem.

Excerpt One

Marielena is explaining the lessons she is trying to teach to her daughter. She sounds

- **a.** angry because other people are constantly telling her daughter what she should be doing.
- **b.** confused about the choices that her daughter is facing.
- **c.** serious about teaching her daughter to find interests that will make her happy.

Excerpt Two

Marielena is discussing her friend, who is changing careers. She sounds

- **a.** amused by the situation her friend is in.
- **b.** ambivalent about her friend's choices in life.
- **c.** frustrated by other people's reaction to her friend's new career.

Excerpt Three

Dan is discussing his expectations for his own life. He sounds

- **a.** unsure about what the future will bring.
- **b.** thoughtful about his responsibilities as a young adult.
- **c.** annoyed because the economic situation makes life very difficult for him.

Excerpt Four

Dan is talking about his part-time job at the bookstore. He sounds

- **a.** concerned that his job is taking time away from his personal life.
- **b.** curious about the impact that his job will have on his life.
- **c.** realistic about the choices that he is making by having a part-time job.

B Listen to the excerpts and circle the letter of the phrase that correctly completes each stem. Compare your answers with a partner.

1 Examining vocabulary in context 🅥

Here are some words and phrases from the interview with Pauline, printed in **bold** and given in the context in which you will hear them. They are followed by definitions.

> I think a lot of people are cold and **distant**: *quiet*; *not wanting to communicate with others*
>
> Modern society values **extroverts** . . . : *people who are social, outgoing, and expressive*
>
> . . . more than **introverts**: *people who are focused on their own thoughts and feelings (as opposed to being interested in social interaction)*
>
> My boss told everyone that they had to be **assertive**: *confident and forceful*
>
> I don't say anything because I need more time to **think things through**: *think carefully about a situation*
>
> My boss put me **on the spot**: *in a difficult or embarrassing situation*
>
> I couldn't think of what to say **right then and there**: *at that particular moment*

2 Listening for main ideas 🅛

A Read the questions before you listen to the interview with Pauline.

1. Many people say that it is important to be independent. Does Pauline agree?
   a. Yes, she does.   **b.** No, she doesn't.   **c.** She's not sure.

2. Pauline says that being independent is not the same as being
   a. responsible and self-sufficient.   **b.** cold and distant.   **c.** efficient and hardworking.

3. What is Pauline's relationship with her neighbors?
   a. They hardly know each other.   **b.** They often visit each other.
   c. They are good friends.

4. What does Pauline say about her work environment?
   a. People work alone.   **b.** People are expected to say what they think.
   c. People work well together.

5. How does Pauline describe her personality?
   a. She is very quiet.   **b.** She likes to speak up.
   c. She thinks before she speaks.

6. At school, many students call their teachers by their first name. What does Pauline think of this?
   a. It is shocking.   **b.** She likes that custom.   **c.** She thinks it is disrespectful.

7. What does Pauline think that men should wear to the opera?
   a. ties and jackets   **b.** jeans and T-shirts   **c.** hats and suits

🔊 **B** Now listen to the interview and circle the correct answers in Step A. Compare answers with a partner.

Sharing your opinion ⓢ

Work with a partner and read about the following situations. Describe how you would react in each situation. What would you say?

I. Your neighbor knocks on your door and asks:

1. "I'm going away for the week. Do you think you could pick up my mail?"

2. "I'm sorry to bother you, but I've locked myself out. Could I please use your phone?"

3. "Sorry, but I'm cooking and I've run out of butter. Do you have a little I could have?"

4. "I'm not going to be home for a couple of weeks. If I give you my key, would you water my plants?"

5. "Is it OK if the mail carrier leaves a package with you tomorrow? I won't be home."

6. "Sorry to bother you, but could I borrow your car for an hour to pick my brother up from the station?"

7. "Could you keep an eye on my kids for an hour or two?"

II. Your friend is coming over to your house for a special dinner party. He/She calls and asks:

1. "I might be a little late. Is that OK?"

2. "I am following a special diet. Would you mind making a few dishes without any meat?"

3. "My elderly aunt and uncle are coming into town. Can you pick them up at the station? I would but I don't have a car."

4. "There's going to be a storm tonight, and my dog gets scared when he hears thunder. Can I bring him to the party?"

5. "After dinner, I don't want to drive home. Is there any way I can stay over?"

6. "I don't like driving home in the dark. Do you think you could drive me home after dinner?"

7. "I'll be coming straight from work. Is it all right if I come a few hours early?"

3 In Your Own Voice

You learned about proverbs and traditional sayings earlier in this chapter. In this section, you will read some other English sayings and discuss the values that they represent.

Sharing your opinion Ⓢ

A Work with a partner. Read the list of sayings below and look up any words you do not know in a dictionary. Then write an explanation of each saying.

1. Money is the root of all evil.

_____

2. Always stand on your own two feet.

_____

3. If at first you don't succeed, try, try again.

_____

4. When in Rome, do as the Romans do.

_____

5. When life gives you lemons, make lemonade.

_____

6. You reap what you sow.

_____

7. Tomorrow is another day.

_____

8. Where there's smoke, there's fire.

_____

9. Don't judge a book by its cover.

_____

10. Haste makes waste.

_____

B With your partner, discuss one of the sayings that you agree or disagree with.

- Explain what the saying means in your own words.
- Say which value(s) the saying suggests.
- Say why you agree or disagree with the saying.
- Tell a story or give an example from your experience that illustrates the saying.

4 Academic Listening and Note Taking

In this section, you will hear and take notes on a two-part lecture given by Harry Peterson, a professor of American studies. The title of his lecture is "Three American Folk Heroes." A *folk hero* can be real, like Steve Jobs, or fictional, like Superman. Folk heroes do extraordinary things. In some cases, they have extraordinary powers that help people. Professor Peterson explains how these heroes represent many important American values. In the second part of the lecture, he answers questions from students.

BEFORE THE LECTURE

1 Sharing your knowledge Ⓢ

The pictures below show three types of American folk heroes. Work in small groups. Look at each picture and discuss the following questions.

　　1. What adjectives can you use to describe this person or character?

　　2. What values does this person or character represent?

　　3. Why do many Americans think of this kind of person or character as a hero?

2 Listening for key words Ⓛ Ⓝ Ⓢ

Key words are the words and expressions that tell you which topic a speaker is discussing. You can recognize these important terms in several ways:

Key words are often repeated:
*So let's begin with the **cowboy**. Think about all the places you see **cowboys**. If you turn on the TV, I guarantee you'll find a **cowboy** movie on one of the channels! And the image of the **cowboy** is also seen constantly in advertising and fashion.*

Key words are often stressed:
*Let's begin with the **COWBOY**.*

🔊 **A** Watch or listen to some parts of the lecture that include key words. As you listen, fill in
🎥 the blanks with the key words you hear.

1. This afternoon, I'm going to talk about three traditional American _____ .
   And by _____ , I mean real people or imaginary figures who do extraordinary
   things or have extraordinary powers.

2. So let's begin with the _____ . Think about all the places you see _____ .
   If you turn on the TV, I guarantee you'll find a _____ movie on one of the
   channels! And the image of the _____ is also seen constantly in advertising and
   fashion.

3. An _____ is a person who starts a company – who makes business deals in
   order to make a profit. We think of _____ as people who have great ideas and
   take risks. And the _____ is also a very powerful symbol of American values.

4. There are all kinds of _____ : Superman, Batman, Wonder Woman, and
   so on. Most _____ have extraordinary powers even though they are in some
   ways very human.

B Work with a partner and compare answers.

C With your partner, take turns reading the items in Step A aloud. Make sure to stress the
words in the blanks.

LECTURE PART 1   Cowboys and Entrepreneurs

1 Guessing vocabulary from context Ⓥ

A The following items contain important vocabulary from Part 1 of the lecture. Work with
a partner. Using the context and your knowledge of related words, take turns guessing
the meanings of the words in **bold**.

_____ 1. Folk heroes are real people who do **extraordinary** things or have
extraordinary powers.

_____ 2. During the nineteenth century, people began moving west in order to **make
their fortune**.

_____ 3. Some of these settlers started large **cattle ranches**.

_____ 4. The cowboy represents courage, freedom, and **independence**.

_____ 5. We think of entrepreneurs as people who have great ideas and **take risks**.

_____ 6. The last American hero I'd like you to think about is **imaginary**.

_____ 7. Most Americans **relate** very strongly **to** the values that the superhero
represents.

B Work with your partner. Match the vocabulary terms in Step A with their definitions below. Write the letters in the blanks next to the sentence or phrase containing the correct term in Step A. Check your answers in a dictionary if necessary.

a. very unusual and special

b. feel strongly connected with

c. do something when there is the possibility of danger or failure

d. ability to do things for yourself

e. not real

f. large areas of land where people raise cows for food

g. become rich and successful

2 Clarifying your notes

> You may find that there are parts of a lecture that you cannot understand because the speaker is talking too quickly. This often happens during a lecture, so do not panic! As you are taking notes, develop a system for marking ideas or words that you need to check. For example, you can use circles, question marks, or asterisks (*) to mark parts that you do not understand. You can also write short questions to yourself or insert a blank line when you have missed an important point.
>
> If possible, clarify any information that you do not understand during the lecture. Most lecturers will encourage you to ask questions. After the lecture, review your notes and ask the lecturer or a classmate about anything that still is not clear.

A Look at a student's notes on the beginning of Professor Peterson's lecture. The circles, question marks, and asterisks indicate things that the student did not understand.

Intro	
Topic: 3 folk heroes = people or ???	missing info.
Do extraord. things or have extraord. powers	sp?
3 famous ones = cowboy, ???, + superhero	
Rep. our most im. values	
1. Cowboy	
See everywhere: TV, ads, fashion	
Why so popular?	missing info.
150 years ago, people moved west to make ?	
Some started catel (sp?) ranches, hired c'boys to help	independent? sp?
C'boy became hero b/c work alone, self-relant*	
Cowboy rep' values: _____ , freedom, _____	

B Copy the notes above onto your own paper. Then watch or listen to Part 1 of the lecture. Listen for the information missing from the student's notes and fill it in. Then continue taking notes on the rest of Part 1. Use circles, question marks, asterisks, blank spaces, and questions to mark parts of the lecture you did not understand.

C Work in small groups. Review and clarify your notes by asking your classmates questions about the parts you marked. Listen to the lecture again if necessary.

D Copy your notes neatly, using any format you prefer.

LECTURE PART 2   Questions and Answers

1 Guessing vocabulary from context Ⓥ

A The following movie review contains important vocabulary from Part 2 of the lecture. Work with a partner. Using the context and your knowledge of related words, take turns guessing the meanings of the words in **bold**.

> The movie *Men of Steel* opened this week to rave reviews. It is a family drama set in America's past during a period of huge industrial (1) **expansion**, and it depicts the everyday struggles of problems faced in steel (2) **factories** in the Midwest.
> The movie focuses on the lives of a father and son who accidentally discover they are heirs to a large amount of money, but decide to give it all away to different (3) **charities**. Despite their riches, they continue to work hard all their lives.
>
> One of the reasons the movie is so satisfying is that the main characters (4) **exemplify** a lot of the values we believe in, like hard work and honesty. No wonder this has become one of the most (5) **profitable** films this year. (6) **Incidentally**, there is a surprise twist at the end of the movie. I wouldn't be surprised if we saw a (7) **sequel** next year!

B Work with your partner. Match the vocabulary terms from Step A with their definitions below. Write the number on the line. Check your answers in a dictionary if necessary.

_____ **a.** organizations that give money or help to people who need it

_____ **b.** buildings where people use machines to make products

_____ **c.** a work that develops the same theme as an earlier one

_____ **d.** growth, increase in number

_____ **e.** making a lot of money

_____ **f.** by the way

_____ **g.** are a typical example of

2 Taking notes on questions and answers

It is common for lecturers to ask students if they have any questions or comments. At this time, you can ask the lecturer to explain ideas that you did not understand. You can also request additional information or make a comment.

Pay attention when your classmates ask questions and listen carefully to the lecturer's answers. Take notes on new information you hear.

A Work with a partner. Read the following questions from Part 2 of the lecture and try to predict Professor Peterson's answers.

1. Could you explain a little more about entrepreneurs?

2. Are there any more modern entrepreneurs that have this "hero quality" you've been describing?

3. I'm really interested in where these values come from, so can you talk a bit more about Superman? Did the Superman figure come out in the nineteenth century?

4. You didn't mention almost any women folk heroes. Why not?

B Now watch or listen to Part 2 of the lecture. As you listen, take notes on the lecturer's responses to the questions.

C Work with a partner and clarify your notes as needed. Then rewrite them neatly and add them to your notes from Part 1.

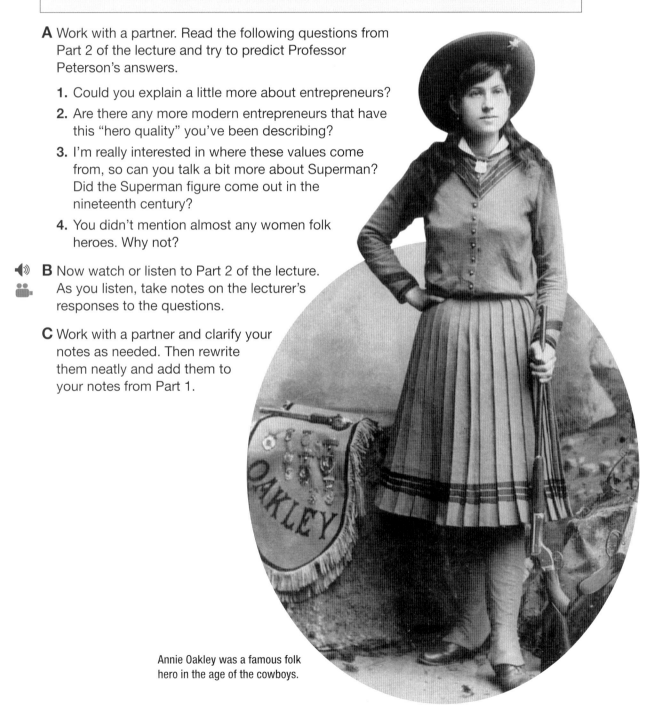

Annie Oakley was a famous folk hero in the age of the cowboys.

Sharing your opinion ⑤

A Read the following true stories. Take notes on the values that you think the people in these stories have. You may list values from this chapter or other values that you think are appropriate.

1. Victoria Ruvolo, a 44-year-old woman, was driving on a highway when some teenagers threw a frozen turkey at her car. The turkey went through the windshield, and she suffered very serious injuries. When she recovered and met her 18-year-old attacker in court, she hugged him. She told him to do good things with his life and persuaded the judge not to send him to prison for 25 years.

2. Police officer Rocco Marini heard on the police radio that a pregnant woman was about to have a baby. He ran out of the station, drove to her home, and delivered a healthy baby boy in her living room. He said it was a really nice feeling to be able to help the new mother.

3. Haider Sediqi, a cab driver in Los Angeles, found $350,000 worth of jewelry in his taxicab. He returned the jewelry to the owner, who rewarded him by sending him a check for $10,000 and a diamond bracelet.

4. Jane Tomlinson, an amateur athlete, raised millions of dollars for charity by competing in demanding athletic challenges, like marathons, triathlons, and long-distance bicycle rides. She continued to do this even after she was diagnosed with terminal cancer. She called her memoir *You Can't Take It with You*.

5. Wesley Autry, a 50-year-old construction worker, was waiting for the New York subway with his two young daughters when a man nearby collapsed and fell onto the tracks in the path of an approaching train. Autry told his girls to stay where they were, jumped down onto the tracks, and held the man flat on the ground, covering him with his body. The train rolled over them, one-half inch above Autry's head. Both men escaped without serious injuries.

B Work with a partner. Discuss your reactions to the stories and compare the values you identified for each person.

C Tell your partner a story about your personal hero or a person who inspired you in some way. What did this person do? What values does the person have?

Chapter 8
American Values Today

Look at the photograph and answer the questions with a partner.

1. What does the photo show? Who are these people, and what are they doing?
2. Do you think this shows a typical situation? How does this family differ from families in the past?

1 Getting Started

In this section, you will read some information about the contrasting values of different groups of Americans. You will also listen to information about a young generation of Americans.

1 Reading and thinking about the topic Ⓥ Ⓢ

A Read the following passage.

Most Americans today believe in traditional values like the importance of freedom and hard work. However, different groups do not always value these things to the same degree. There are often differences of opinion between generations because of their different life experiences. For example, the *Greatest Generation* – people born before 1928 – had differences of opinion from the *Silent Generation* – people born between 1928 and 1945. More recently, *Baby Boomers* – people born between the end of World War II and the mid-1960s – had different experiences from *Generation X*, people born between the mid-1960s and the 1970s or from *Generation Y* (also called the *Millennial Generation*), people born during the late 1970s and the 1980s. Experts do not agree on the exact beginning and ending years of these generations, but it is certain that world events and technological innovations during these people's lives shaped their values in different ways.

Like people all over the world, Americans do not all share the same political views. Some are more *conservative*, meaning that they tend to believe in keeping traditional cultural and religious values and oppose sudden change. Other Americans are more *liberal*, meaning that they tend to favor reform and progress more than tradition. These different political philosophies often lead to disagreements among Americans about important issues, such as the role of government, taxes, and immigration.

B Answer the following questions according to the information in the passage.

1. What are the five generations of Americans that the passage describes?
2. Why do these five generations often have different values?
3. What do conservatives tend to believe? What beliefs do liberals tend to share?

C Read these questions and share your responses with a partner:

1. Do you think young people always have values that are different from values of older people?
2. Are there some values that you think will never change? If so, what are they? Why won't they change?

2 Sharing your knowledge ⑤

Baby Boomer

Generation X

Generation Y

A Look at the pictures above. Which of the following items were important (or started to become important) when these people were young? Write *BB* (Baby Boomer), *X* (Generation X), or *Y* (Generation Y) on the lines.

1. Important event   _____ **a.** The World Trade Center in New York was attacked.

         _____ **b.** The Soviet Union broke up, and the Berlin Wall fell.

         _____ **c.** The Vietnam War took place.

2. Important music and musicians   _____ **a.** rock 'n' roll

         _____ **b.** disco/pop

         _____ **c.** hip-hop

3. Important technology   _____ **a.** iPads

         _____ **b.** TVs

         _____ **c.** computers

B Discuss the following questions as a class.

1. What additional information do you know about these three generations?

2. How do you think the different experiences of these generations affected their values?

3 Listening for specific information ⓛ ⓝ ⓢ

A You will hear a conversation about Generation Y. Look at the chart below and notice the information you need to listen for. Then work with a partner and try to predict the information you will hear.

Information to listen for	Notes
Size of Generation Y	
Percentage of U.S. population	
Six times as big as:	
Values of Generation Y	

B Now listen to the conversation and take notes in the right column.

C Work with a partner and compare your answers. Then discuss the following questions.

1. Are you, or someone you know well, a member of Generation Y? Do you or the other person you know have the same values as the man in the conversation?

2. What are some other values of this generation?

3. Think about people who belong to Generation Y in other countries you know. Do they have the same values as the man in the conversation?

4. What problems do members of Generation Y face?

2 Real-Life Voices

In this section, you will hear several Americans talking about their values. First, you will listen to three young adults – Rosiane, Benjamin, and Christine – talk about differences between their values and the values of their parents. Then you will hear an interview with Sandra, who is in her 50s. In the interview, Sandra talks about values and behavior that she thinks young people need in order to succeed in the workplace.

BEFORE THE INTERVIEWS

Sharing your opinion ⓢ

What are your most important values? Are they the same as your parents' or different? Fill in the Venn diagram below with examples of your values, your parents' values, and values that you and your parents share. Then compare your answers in small groups.

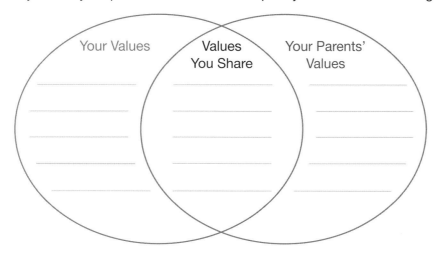

Your Values | Values You Share | Your Parents' Values

INTERVIEW 1   Differences in Values Between Parents and Children

1 Examining vocabulary in context ⓥ

Here are some words and phrases from the interview with Rosiane, Benjamin, and Christine, printed in **bold** and given in the context in which you will hear them. They are followed by definitions.

> They wanted me to . . . have kids, so that they could help **bring up** the grandchildren: *raise*
>
> I guess I was more **adventurous**: *willing to take risks*
>
> What do your parents think about your **choices**?: *the decisions you made*
>
> I think **I see eye to eye** with my parents: *agree with*
>
> Perhaps that's a kind of **pejorative** expression: *disapproving, insulting*
>
> Your parents don't need to keep constantly **hovering over you**: *watching everything you do*
>
> I think . . . traveling makes you more **open-minded**: *tolerant, able to accept different opinions*

2 Drawing inferences Ⓢ Ⓛ

🔊 **A** Read the questions below. Then listen to the interviews and write *R* (Rosiane), *B* (Benjamin), or *C* (Christine) on the lines. After you listen, check your answers with a partner.

1. Who thinks it is important to . . .

_____ **a.** be adventurous?

_____ **b.** live abroad?

_____ **c.** travel?

_____ **d.** have more independence from parents?

_____ **e.** find a career before getting married?

_____ **f.** have more privacy?

2. Whose parents wanted their child to . . .

_____ **a.** get married at a young age?

_____ **b.** stay in the town where they live?

_____ **c.** follow their advice about homework and course choices?

B Work with a partner. Read the e-mails below and discuss which of the following people might have written them. Write the name of the person in the blank.

Rosiane   Benjamin   Christine

Rosiane's father   Benjamin's mother   Christine's mother

1. 🔴🔴🔴

Hi Angela!

I'm really excited – I just got offered a job in Chile, and I desperately want to go. There's just one thing I'm worried about, and that's my parents' reaction. They want me to settle down close to home. I'm not sure how I'm going to handle this. Can we have lunch soon?

_____

2. 🔴🔴🔴

Hello, Paul dear,

How are you? I hear you've been having some trouble at work. Listen, sweetie, try not to get too upset about things. I know your boss is kind of demanding, but you have to be your own man. You can't let other people tell you what to do all the time.

_____

3. 🔴🔴🔴

Hi Nancy,

How are you? Do you want to get together? I've hardly seen anyone since I got married. It's getting difficult to juggle my work, the house, and fun! Everything is going well at home, but it would be great to see you again and catch up on what you're doing. Write back soon!

_____

4. 🔴🔴🔴

Dear Frank,

I'm writing to ask for your advice. My daughter has a job offer in South America, and she's talking about moving there. What am I supposed to tell her? If she moves abroad, I'll never get to see her!

_____

5.

Hi Paul,

Mom told me your boss has been putting a lot of pressure on you. Don't worry too much. And don't get mad at mom, OK? I know she interferes a lot, but she just wants the best for you! (Well, at least she's focusing on you right now and leaving me alone ☺ ...)

6.

Hello Bert,

I'm just writing to catch up. We haven't been in touch lately, but I've got some great news – my daughter finally got married! I thought that was never going to happen! Now let's see how many more years it will take me to become a grandparent!

C Work with a partner and discuss the e-mails. Which values do you think the writers of the e-mails demonstrate?

3 Listening for stressed words ①

> When speakers are comparing two ideas, they often stress two words that show the contrast they are making.
>
> **Example:**
> *Even though **MY** values are different from **THEIRS**, they accepted my decisions.*
> Rosiane is contrasting her values with her family's values.

◀》 **A** Listen to the excerpts from the interview. Circle the correct answers.

Excerpt One

Rosiane is discussing her goals when she was younger. The two words she stresses are:

   a. husband, career

   b. my, early

   c. wasn't looking, was busy

Excerpt Two

Benjamin is talking about differences between him and his parents. The two words he stresses are:

   a. I, they

   b. respect, need

   c. opinions, privacy

Excerpt Three

Christine is talking about her parents' attitude toward her life. The two words she stresses are:

   a. open, change

   b. really, but

   c. I'm, aren't

B Look again at the answers. With a partner, explain the contrast that the speakers are making.

INTERVIEW 2   Values in the Workplace

1 Examining vocabulary in context ⓥ

Here are some words and phrases from the interview with Sandra, printed in **bold** and given in the context in which you will hear them. They are followed by definitions.

I find that sometimes, students don't respect **deadlines** . . . : *the date when a task or an assignment must be completed*

They think, "Well, I don't have to **submit** my paper on time": *give the paper to the professor*

But they have to learn that that is not **acceptable**: *satisfactory*

And you go to the **dealer**, and everything is all paid for: *salesperson*

You're going to be really **upset**: *angry and unhappy*

They want to **stand out**: *appear to be special or better than anyone else*

You don't work **in isolation**: *alone*

But don't you think individual **effort** is important?: *physical or mental activity needed in order to achieve something*

2 Listening for specific information Ⓛ Ⓝ Ⓢ

🔊 **A** Read the questions below before you listen to the interview with Sandra. Then listen and take notes on the answers.

1. What is Sandra's job? _____

_____

2. What question does she ask her students? _____

_____

3. Why does she say it is important for students to respect deadlines? _____

_____

4. What story does she tell to show them the importance of time? _____

_____

5. What is the second value she teaches them, and why is it important? _____

_____

6. Which examples does she give of the importance of professionalism? _____

_____

B Work with a partner and compare answers.

3 Role-playing ⓢ

A With your partner, read the comments Sandra hears from students who come to talk to her in her office. Discuss how she would probably respond.

1. "Good morning, Professor. I'm sorry to bother you. I know you've assigned a group project for next week, but I prefer to work alone. Is that possible?"

2. "Hello, Professor, I have a question I need to ask you. I'm almost finished with my term paper, but I need a little bit more time. Could I please turn it in a few days late?"

3. "Hey, Prof. Listen, I'm really sorry, but I won't be able to make it to class this afternoon 'cos you know, uh, something's come up. But . . . uh . . . I'll be there next week, OK?"

B Practice role-playing the conversations in Step A with your partner. You can expand on the conversation and add more details. Then choose one of your role plays and perform it for another pair of students. Listen as they do their role play for you.

AFTER THE INTERVIEWS

Sharing your opinion ⓢ

A Read the following statements. For each statement, decide whether you strongly agree, agree, aren't sure, disagree, or strongly disagree. Circle the words that show your opinion. Make notes about your reasons.

1. It is important for both men and women to have a career before getting married.

   Strongly agree   Agree   Not sure   Disagree   Strongly disagree

   Reason: _____

2. Young adults should follow their parents' advice about important decisions in their lives.

   Strongly agree   Agree   Not sure   Disagree   Strongly disagree

   Reason: _____

3. It is important for people to travel to other countries.

   Strongly agree   Agree   Not sure   Disagree   Strongly disagree

   Reason: _____

4. Children need strong discipline.

   Strongly agree   Agree   Not sure   Disagree   Strongly disagree

   Reason: _____

5. It should be against the law to spank children.

   Strongly agree   Agree   Not sure   Disagree   Strongly disagree

   Reason: _____

6. Cooperation is more important than individual effort in the workplace.

   Strongly agree   Agree   Not sure   Disagree   Strongly disagree

   Reason: _____

B Work with a partner and explain your responses.

3 In Your Own Voice

In this section, you will conduct a short survey to find out what people think is important in a job. Then you will share your findings with a small group.

Conducting a survey Ⓢ

A Numerous studies of the Millennial Generation are reaching similar conclusions about its values. The studies suggest that Millennials are different from their parents. They tend to be more confident, self-expressive, open to change, and connected with others. These characteristics have become very important as the Millennials grow up and enter the workplace. Read about their characteristics in the chart below.

Millennials have the following characteristics. They . . .	Examples
want to "be themselves" at work.	93% want to dress whatever way they like. They do not like having to follow a "dress code." In fact, they like to be very informal.
like to be connected with others.	83% of them sleep with their cell phones. They feel it is important to be able to communicate with others at all times.
are concerned about being responsible.	80% say they want feedback from their bosses. They want to make sure they do their best.
value self-expression.	75% of them have a profile on a social network. They update their profile frequently and tell others about their lives.
don't think a high salary is the number-one priority in a job.	Less than 25% say that having a high-paying career is very important to them.
have strong ideas about fashion.	40% have tattoos (and most of those have more than one).

B Interview at least three people outside your class who are Millennials. Follow these steps.

1. Use the chart on the next page for your survey, or make a chart of your own.

2. Circle "Male" or "Female" for each interviewee. Then ask them to talk about their opinions. Here is an example of how to start:

   Excuse me. I'm conducting a survey for my English class. It's about personal characteristics that affect people's lives and their jobs. Do you have time to answer a few questions for me?

3. Check [✓] each response in the appropriate column. If you need to, you can read the interviewees the examples from the chart above.

4. Ask follow-up questions. Ask the interviewees to explain their answers. Take notes on what they say.

Personal Characteristics						
Do you . . .	Person 1: Name/Age		Person 2: Name/Age		Person 3: Name/Age	
	Male / Female		Male / Female		Male / Female	
	Yes	No	Yes	No	Yes	No
1. want to "be yourself" at work?						
2. like to be connected with others?						
3. want feedback from your boss at work?						
4. value self-expression?						
5. think having a high-paying job is one of your top priorities?						
6. have strong ideas about fashion?						
Notes:						

C Answer the following questions.

1. Did you find any similarities or differences between people's opinions? What were they?

2. What was the most interesting answer the speakers gave to your follow-up questions?

3. Work in small groups and compare your answers.

4 Academic Listening and Note Taking

In this section, you will hear and take notes on a two-part lecture given by Jason LaRose, a professor of political science. The title of his lecture is "Conservative and Liberal Values in American Politics." Professor LaRose will discuss these values and their relationship to the two main political parties in the United States.

BEFORE THE LECTURE

1 Building background knowledge on the topic Ⓥ

A In this task, you will learn some facts about the two main political parties in the United States, the Democratic Party and the Republican Party.

Work with a partner.

Partner A, look at the chart below on this page.

Partner B, look at the chart at the top of the next page.

B Ask your partner questions about the information that is missing from your chart. Fill in the blanks with information your partner gives you. Then answer your partner's questions. Here is an example:

A: *What is the color of the Republican Party?*

B: *Red. What is the symbol of the Democratic Party?*

A: *A donkey.*

Partner A

Facts	Democratic Party	Republican Party
Political philosophy	liberalism	
Color	blue	
Symbol	donkey	
Web site	www.democrats.org	
Interesting fact	the first party to nominate a woman for vice president	
Some well-known presidents	Franklin D. Roosevelt John F. Kennedy Lyndon B. Johnson William Clinton Barack Obama	

Partner B

Facts	Republican Party	Democratic Party
Political philosophy	conservatism	
Color	red	
Symbol	elephant	
Web site	www.gop.com	
Interesting fact	commonly called the GOP (Grand Old Party)	
Some well-known presidents	Dwight Eisenhower Richard Nixon Ronald Reagan George W. Bush	

2 Listening for general statements Ⓛ Ⓝ

It is common in a short lecture for the speaker to make general statements about a topic because there is not enough time to give detailed information. Here are some words and phrases that are often used to make general statements:

generally   in general   commonly   many
most   often   typically   usually

A Read the statements below. Notice that they do not use any of the words and phrases from the box.

_____ **1.** But even though people's values are very diverse, the strongest voices in American politics today do fall into two groups: conservative and liberal.

_____ **2.** Conservatives put a strong emphasis on personal responsibility.

_____ **3.** Liberals, on the other hand, think the government should be very active in fixing social problems like poverty and illness.

_____ **4.** Conservatives think government is too big and expensive.

_____ **5.** Conservatives believe that the government should stay out of the way of business.

_____ **6.** Liberals believe that government should control and regulate business through strict laws or taxes.

B Now watch or listen to the statements with words and phrases that signal general statements. Write the signal word or phrase you hear next to each statement in Step A.

C Work with a partner and compare your answers. Discuss the difference in meaning between the sentences in Step A and in Step B.

LECTURE PART 1 Conservative and Liberal Values

1 Guessing vocabulary from context ⓥ

A The following items contain important vocabulary from Part 1 of the lecture. Work with a partner. Using the context and your knowledge of related words, take turns guessing the meanings of the words in **bold**.

_____ **1.** So let me outline for you some basic differences between conservatives and liberals in three areas: the role of the government, taxes, and government **regulation** of business.

_____ **2.** Conservatives usually put a strong **emphasis** on personal responsibility.

_____ **3.** They don't believe it's the government's responsibility to pay for social programs that guarantee things like a **minimum wage**.

_____ **4.** Most liberals think the government should be very active in fixing social problems like **poverty** and illness.

_____ **5.** Conservatives believe that the government shouldn't **interfere** too much in the way business works.

_____ **6.** They think entrepreneurs won't care about their workers or their customers or the **environment**.

_____ **7.** They'll only care about their own **profits**.

B Work with your partner. Match the vocabulary terms from Step A with their definitions below. Write the letters in the blanks next to the sentence or phrase containing the correct term in Step A. Check your answers in a dictionary if necessary.

a. special attention that is given to something because it is important

b. the condition of being poor

c. money that a business makes

d. participate without being wanted or asked to do so

e. control of, rules on

f. the lowest salary that a business is allowed by law to pay its employees

g. the natural world around us, nature

2 Taking notes in a point-by-point format Ⓝ Ⓛ

When lecturers compare two or more groups, they often use a "point-by-point" format to organize their ideas. Here are some examples:

Topics (points)	Groups compared
1. Attitudes toward marriage	Older people
	Younger people
2. Attitudes about money	Men
	Women
3. Voting patterns	Liberals
	Conservatives

A Look at the incomplete notes for Part 1 of the lecture. Predict the information you need to listen for.

Conserv/Lib Values

1. Role of gov't   Conserv: Not govt. resp. to pay for social progs

                          Lib: Gov't should fix soc. probs like poverty and illness

2. _____   _____

                          _____

3. _____   _____

                          _____

                          Ex: _____

B Now watch or listen to Part 1 of the lecture and take notes on your own paper. Use a point-by-point format like the one above.

C Work with a partner and compare your notes. Then use your notes to fill in the missing information in Step A.

1 Guessing vocabulary from context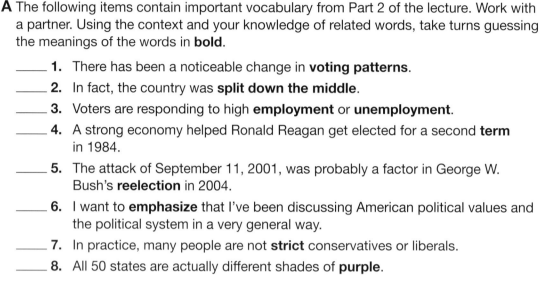

A The following items contain important vocabulary from Part 2 of the lecture. Work with a partner. Using the context and your knowledge of related words, take turns guessing the meanings of the words in **bold**.

_____ **1.** There has been a noticeable change in **voting patterns**.

_____ **2.** In fact, the country was **split down the middle**.

_____ **3.** Voters are responding to high **employment** or **unemployment**.

_____ **4.** A strong economy helped Ronald Reagan get elected for a second **term** in 1984.

_____ **5.** The attack of September 11, 2001, was probably a factor in George W. Bush's **reelection** in 2004.

_____ **6.** I want to **emphasize** that I've been discussing American political values and the political system in a very general way.

_____ **7.** In practice, many people are not **strict** conservatives or liberals.

_____ **8.** All 50 states are actually different shades of **purple**.

B Work with your partner. Match the vocabulary terms in Step A with their definitions below. Write the letters in the blanks next to the sentence or phrase containing the correct term in Step A. Check your answers in a dictionary if necessary.

a. divided half and half

b. the usual or normal way that most people vote

c. the percentage of people who have (or don't have) work

d. a mixture of red and blue

e. say strongly, stress

f. 100 percent, completely

g. winning an election for the second time

h. the period of time an elected official serves

2 Using information on the board to help you take notes

> Lecturers sometimes write important information on the board to help students understand what they are saying. If this happens, pay close attention to the information and use it to make predictions, learn new vocabulary, or write comments or questions about anything that you do not understand.

A Look at the information that Professor LaRose wrote on the board. Then study the incomplete notes for Part 2 of the lecture. Predict the information you need to listen for.

U.S. Presidents of Recent History

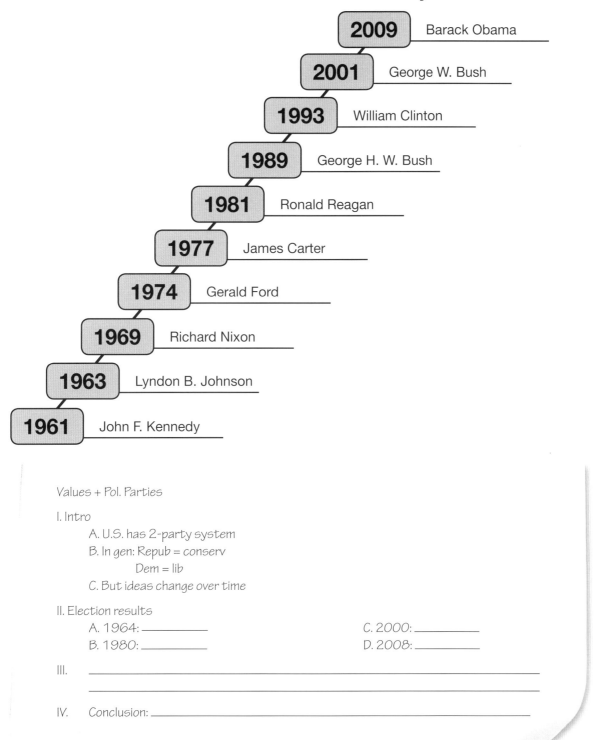

2009 Barack Obama

2001 George W. Bush

1993 William Clinton

1989 George H. W. Bush

1981 Ronald Reagan

1977 James Carter

1974 Gerald Ford

1969 Richard Nixon

1963 Lyndon B. Johnson

1961 John F. Kennedy

Values + Pol. Parties

I. Intro
    A. U.S. has 2-party system
    B. In gen: Repub = conserv
          Dem = lib
    C. But ideas change over time

II. Election results
    A. 1964: _____   C. 2000: _____
    B. 1980: _____   D. 2008: _____

III. _____
_____

IV. Conclusion: _____

B Now watch or listen to Part 2 of the lecture and take notes on your own paper.

C Compare your notes with a partner. Then use your notes to fill in the missing information in Step A.

Sharing your opinion Ⓢ

A Are you more liberal or more conservative? Take the quiz below to find out!
Read each statement and circle *Agree*, *Not Sure*, or *Disagree* to indicate your opinions.

1. We must protect our natural resources (forests, rivers, lakes, etc.) even if this means we must limit business activities in these areas.

   Agree   Not sure   Disagree

2. The government should restrict immigration to the United States.

   Agree   Not sure   Disagree

3. Businesses should give preference to members of minority groups in their employment policies because they were treated unfairly in the past.

   Agree   Not sure   Disagree

4. Carrying a gun is an American right.

   Agree   Not sure   Disagree

5. It is important for the government to provide access to health care even if this means increasing taxes.

   Agree   Not sure   Disagree

6. In some cases, death is the right punishment for criminals.

   Agree   Not sure   Disagree

7. The government should provide equal access to a good education for all its citizens.

   Agree   Not sure   Disagree

8. Taxes should be cut if it will help the economy to grow.

   Agree   Not sure   Disagree

B Score your quiz. Give yourself points and write an *X* on the scale to show how your views compare with the views of liberal and conservative Americans.

| Odd numbers (1, 3, 5, 7): | Agree = 0, Not sure = 1, Disagree = 2 |
| Even numbers (2, 4, 6, 8): | Agree = 2, Not sure = 1, Disagree = 0 |

0   16

More liberal   More conservative

C Work with a partner or small group. Compare and discuss your responses to the statements in Step A.

Unit 4 Academic Vocabulary Review

This section reviews the vocabulary from Chapters 7 and 8. For a complete list of the Academic Word List words in this book, see the Appendix on page 182.

A Look at the list of words. Write the part(s) of speech each word represents: *V* for verb, *A* for adjective, *N* for noun, or *O* for other. Use your dictionary if necessary. Then compare your answers with the class.

Academic word	Part of speech
1. appropriate	
2. comment	
3. constant	
4. cooperate	
5. dramatic	
6. emphasize	
7. eventually	
8. generation	

Academic word	Part of speech
9. incidentally	
10. individual	
11. minimum	
12. publish	
13. respond	
14. specific	
15. team	

B Use a form of the words in the box to complete the conversations.

1. At work

Henry: Kenny, do you have a minute? I need to ask you for some advice.

Kenny: Sure, what do you need?

Henry: I'm a bit concerned about my job. My boss is (1) _____ talking about the importance of (2) _____ . She says that she expects us to work as a (3) _____ .

Kenny: That sounds reasonable. What's wrong with that?

Henry: Well, nothing, at least not in theory. But the trouble is that we all work in different ways. Some people like working with others, but I prefer to work alone. I find that if people work (4) _____ , they often come up with better ideas than if they are in a big group.

Kenny: Oh, I see. Well, I don't think you should be so worried. You'll work it all out (5) _____ .

Henry: Well, maybe you're right. Perhaps I shouldn't be so concerned.

> constant
> cooperate
> eventually
> individual
> team

2. At school

Hugh: I'm so angry. I walked into the classroom today and the professor made a strange (1) _____ .

Isabelle: What did he say?

Hugh: He said that Millennials were much too informal. He said that when he was young, students came to class wearing jackets. I was wearing jeans, and I didn't appreciate his sense of humor.

Isabelle: Well, I understand why you're upset. I don't think the professor was being
(2) _____ . What did the other students say?

Hugh: Well, at first nobody wanted to (3) _____ . But then someone said that we should be able to wear whatever we like to class. And the professor said nothing. He just started lecturing.

Isabelle: Well, try to stop thinking about it. He probably didn't mean to insult you – it's just a (4) _____ thing. People were more formal in the past than they are now.

Hugh: Yeah, but he made me feel bad, and I don't think that's right. Oh, and (5) _____ , other students have complained about this professor, too. He speaks before he thinks!

> appropriate
> comment
> generation
> incidentally
> respond

3. On the street

Susie: I can't believe what I just saw outside. Some people were protesting about unemployment, and they were shouting in front of the bank.

Neil: Wow, that sounds pretty (1) _____ . What were they protesting about?

Susie: Well, it was very general. They didn't seem to be saying anything (2) _____ .

Neil: You know, the economic situation is not good right now. I was just reading a government (3) _____ about unemployment. It said that there are more and more young people without a job.

Susie: I know. There should be more (4) _____ on creating new jobs, right?

Neil: Yes – and high-paying jobs. Most of the jobs I've seen only pay the (5) _____ wage.

Susie: Well, I hope the situation gets better soon!

> dramatic
> emphasize
> minimum
> publish
> specific

C Use the academic vocabulary from Step A above to answer the following questions in pairs or as a class.

Personal Values

1. What are the values that Americans consider most important?
2. In what ways do parents teach children about values?
3. What are some sayings that illustrate American values?

American Folk Heroes

4. What are some American folk heroes, and where do we see them?
5. What important values do folk heroes reflect?
6. Where do folk heroes come from?

Contrasting Values

7. What generations does the unit discuss?
8. What are some values of the Millennial Generation?
9. What values are important in the workplace?

Conservative and Liberal Values

10. What are the two main parties in the United States?
11. What issues do these parties often disagree about?
12. How do conservative and liberal values affect politics?

Oral Presentation

You will make a three-minute presentation to the class about important values, issues in politics, or conflicts with others over values.

BEFORE THE PRESENTATION

1 Choose a topic

Choose one of the topics below. Try to choose a topic that is different from the topic chosen by other members of your class.

Important values

- cooperation
- freedom
- gratitude
- honesty
- imagination
- perseverance
- respect
- other (choose your own)

Political issues

- taxes
- environmental protection
- health care
- poverty
- immigration
- transportation
- housing
- other (your own choice)

Conflicts over values

- parents and children
- colleagues
- bosses and employees
- siblings
- neighbors
- friends
- husband and wife
- other (your choice)

2 Prepare your presentation

- Think about why you chose this topic. What makes it interesting for you? What is the main point you would like to make about it?
- Do some research about the topic online, or speak to other people. What do they say that makes it more interesting?
- Think of an anecdote, proverb, story, or joke that illustrates your point. Adding these elements will make your presentation much more interesting for your classmates.
- Practice your presentation in front of a mirror or with your friends and family. Stay within the time limit.

DURING THE PRESENTATION

- Relax, and try to speak naturally. Do not read from your notes.
- Define the topic.

    Example:
    I'm going to talk about an important value: believing in others.
    Believing in others means . . .

- Explain why you think your topic is important.

    Example:
    I think it is very important to provide health care because . . .

- Illustrate your idea with an example or anecdote.

    Example:
    I am going to tell you a story about a conflict between a parent and child . . .

- Pause from time to time and make sure your classmates understand what you are saying.

AFTER THE PRESENTATION

A When you finish your presentation, ask your classmates if they understood your main idea and if they have questions or comments.

B Ask your teacher or your classmates for feedback. You can use a chart like this or make your own.

Grammar	Delivery
Did I make many grammar mistakes? What were they? How can I improve?	Did I speak loudly enough? Did I speak clearly enough? Did I use effective body language?
Pronunciation	**Preparation**
Were there any words I mispronounced? Was my intonation good? Did I speak slowly enough for others to understand?	Was the information correct? Was the information interesting? Did I explain why the topic was important?

C Give your feedback to other classmates. Try to communicate your ideas in a supportive way that will help your classmates improve their oral presentation skills.

Lectures: Video script

Unit 1: Laws of the Land
Chapter 1: The Foundations of Government

Lecture:
"The Structure of the U.S. Federal Government"

Before the Lecture:
Listening for the plan of a lecture, page 14

Hi. Welcome to you all. My name is Nelson Rodgers. I'm here to represent Ed Sullivan, who was an elected official in New York State for many years. Before that, he also taught English for about 15 years, and he loves to teach students about the U.S. government. He sends you his greetings.

You know, whenever I speak to students, I always get a lot of questions about the basic structure of the federal government. So what I'm going to do today is give you an overview of how the government is organized, and that way, you can start to understand how it works. First, I'll introduce the three branches of government. Oh, uh, I'll be using this chart here on the board to help you understand. And then, after that, I'll explain the system of checks and balances.

Lecture Part 1:
"The Three Branches of the U.S. Federal Government"

Using information the lecturer puts on the board, page 17

Hi. Welcome to you all. My name is Nelson Rodgers. I'm here to represent Ed Sullivan, who was an elected official in New York State for many years. Before that, he also taught English for about 15 years, and he loves to teach students about the U.S. government. He sends you his greetings.

You know, whenever I speak to students, I always get a lot of questions about the basic structure of the federal government. So what I'm going to do today is give you an overview of how the government is organized, and that way, you can start to understand how it works. First, I'll introduce the three branches

of government. Oh, uh, I'll be using this chart here on the board to help you understand. And then, after that, I'll explain the system of checks and balances.

All right, now, as you can see on the board, the U.S. government has three branches, or parts, called the legislative, executive, and judicial. So let me start with the legislative branch, which makes the laws. So here on the left, where it says "Responsibility," I'm writing "makes laws." I'll just fill in this box for you as an example. OK. In the U.S., the legislative branch of government is called Congress. And Congress actually has two parts, or houses: the Senate and the House of Representatives. Members of the Senate are called Senators, and members of the House are called Representatives. Have you got that? OK.

Good. So now let me give you a few more details about Congress. Each state has two Senators, and since there are 50 states, there are exactly 100 senators. On the other hand, the House of Representatives has 435 members. That's because the number of representatives from each state depends on the size of that state's population. Obviously, states with larger populations, like California, have more representatives.

All right. The next branch of government I want to describe is the executive branch, which executes, or approves, the laws that Congress makes. And who has that job? The president. Actually the president has many responsibilities, but the most important one is the power to approve laws. Now besides the president, the executive branch also includes the vice president and the heads of government departments, who are called secretaries – you know, Secretary of State, Secretary of Defense, Secretary of Education, and so on.

Finally there's the judicial branch. Judicial is related to the word *judge*. Now, there are three levels of courts in the United States: city, state, and federal. But when we talk about the judicial branch of the federal government, we're usually talking about the Supreme Court, which is the highest court in the land. The Supreme Court has nine members, called justices, and their job is to interpret the laws passed by Congress, in other words, to decide if a law is constitutional or not.

Lecture Part 2:
"The System of Checks and Balances"
Taking good lecture notes, page 18

OK. Now why do you think the federal government is divided this way? Well, the founding fathers, meaning the men who wrote the Constitution, wanted to avoid a dictatorship. They didn't want one person or one branch to have too much power, and to make sure this didn't happen, they invented a system of "checks and balances." Checks and balances means that the three branches of government have separate responsibilities, but they also have the power to check, or limit, each other's actions.

Let me give you some examples of how checks and balances work. The way Supreme Court justices are chosen is a good example. Supreme Court justices don't get elected. The president chooses them. But the Senate has the power to approve or disapprove of the president's choice. The Senate, in this case, can check the president's power to choose Supreme Court justices.

Here's another example. Let's suppose Congress passes a law, but the president doesn't want to approve it. If that happens, the Constitution gives the president the power to veto it – in other words, he can decide not to sign it. And according to the Constitution, a law doesn't become a law until the president signs it. So in this case, the president is checking the power of Congress.

Let me give you a third example. Suppose Congress passes a law and the president signs it. Is that the end of the process? Usually yes, but sometimes no. There are times when people challenge the constitutionality of a law. It can be a private citizen or the corporation or a city government who believes that a law is wrong or unfair because it goes against the Constitution. Most cases like that will be heard in a lower-level court. But the Supreme Court has the final authority to decide if the law – which was passed by Congress and signed by the president, remember – is either constitutional or unconstitutional. So this is an example of the Supreme Court checking and balancing the other two branches.

So I hope now that you have a basic understanding of the three branches of the U.S. government and how these branches control each other through a system of checks and balances.

Chapter 2: Constitutional Issues Today

Lecture:
"The First Amendment"
Before the Lecture:
Listening for main ideas and details, page 32

1. What does it mean to have freedom of religion? Well, freedom of religion is a very important right. Basically it means two things: First, Americans are free to practice their religion without interference from the government, and second, there is no national religion. Now this freedom affects Americans in many ways. For instance, an employer can't hire you or fire you just because he likes or doesn't like your religion. And freedom of religion includes how you dress. What I mean is, Americans are free to wear any kind of religious clothing they prefer.

2. All right. Now, the next freedom listed in the First Amendment is maybe the most famous one, because it's the one that all of us practice every single day, and that's freedom of speech. What does that mean, exactly? Basically, it means you're free to talk openly about your ideas even if other people disagree with them. You're also free to read or listen to other people's ideas. But in addition, freedom of speech includes what we call "symbolic speech" – like wearing the clothes you like. In fact, the courts have said that freedom of speech includes all forms of expression, meaning words, pictures, music . . . even the way you wear your hair!

Lecture Part 1:
"Overview of the First Amendment"
Using symbols and abbreviations, page 33

Today's lecture is about the First Amendment to the U.S . Constitution, which for many Americans is probably the most important part of the Bill of Rights, because it affects the way we live every day. I'll begin with an overview of the five freedoms in the First Amendment, and after that, in the second part of my talk, I'll tell you about some cases that will show you why the First Amendment is so controversial.

So, now the First Amendment guarantees American citizens five basic freedoms: freedom of religion, speech, press, assembly, and petition. What does it mean to have freedom of religion? Well, freedom of religion is a very important right. Basically it means two things: First, Americans are free to practice their religion without interference from the government, and second, there is no national religion. Now this freedom affects Americans in many ways. For instance, an employer can't hire you or fire you just because he likes or doesn't like your religion. And freedom of religion includes how you dress. What I mean is, Americans are free to wear any kind of religious clothing they prefer. For example, some religions require people to cover their heads all the time, while others require people to take their hats off, for example, in church. Both of these forms of expression are legal.

All right. Now, the next freedom listed in the First Amendment is maybe the most famous one, because it's the one that all of us practice every single day, and that's freedom of speech. What does that mean, exactly? Basically, it means you're free to talk openly about your ideas, even if other people disagree with them. You're also free to read or listen to other people's ideas. But in addition, freedom of speech includes what we call "symbolic speech" – like wearing the clothes you like. In fact, the courts have said that freedom of speech includes all forms of expression, meaning words, pictures, music, even the way you wear your hair!

The third freedom, freedom of press, means the freedom to publish books and articles in newspapers, magazines, and even the Internet. Journalists and publishers have the right to publish different ideas and opinions. Let's say you open a magazine, and you see a cartoon making a joke about the president. You might ask yourself: Is that legal? And the answer is yes. It's also perfectly legal for a journalist to write an article criticizing the government. You can open the newspaper any day and find articles that criticize the government for, oh, let's see, raising taxes or not protecting the environment, or, well of course, military activities in other countries. Journalists are free to agree or disagree with these actions and express their opinions without fear.

The First Amendment lists two other freedoms as well: freedom of assembly and freedom of petition. Freedom of assembly means, very simply, the right to meet in groups. When students participate in demonstrations on college campuses, for example, they are using their right of assembly and the right of free speech at the same time.

And the fifth and last freedom is the freedom of petition, which means citizens have the right to ask the government to change laws or change policies. In other words, it means that citizens can complain about the government's actions.

I've listed these five freedoms separately, but in real life, we often use the term "freedom of expression" to talk about all of them. Freedom of expression means the right that Americans have to express their views in any form they prefer, for example, by speaking, writing a letter to their senator, demonstrating in the streets, writing a song, or painting a picture.

Lecture Part 2:
"First Amendment Controversies"
Using a map to organize your notes, page 35

Perhaps you're wondering: Does the First Amendment mean Americans are completely free to say and do whatever they want? And of course the answer is no. There are limits, but trying to decide where and what they are can be very controversial. Let's look at the kinds of questions that our courts deal with all the time.

The first question is: What are the limits of free speech? You see, in practice, there are some restrictions. For example, it's never legal to publish lies about people. But should it be legal to burn the U.S. flag as a form of criticism against the government? Some people say yes because the First Amendment guarantees free expression. But many other people disagree. They think flag burning is unpatriotic and insults the country. You might be surprised to hear that the Supreme Court has ruled that flag burning is legal, but this is very controversial.

Here's another question. Should children be allowed to bring cell phones to school? Many teachers and principals say no, because cell phones make noise in class, and they've tried to forbid cell phones or take them away from children. However, many parents say they need to have a way to get in touch with their children, and they also say that using a cell phone is a form of free speech.

Let's look at another controversial question that often comes up: What does freedom of religion actually mean, in practice? For example, do you think children should have the right to say prayers in public schools? Some people say yes because the First Amendment guarantees freedom of religion, right? But other people say no because the First Amendment also says there cannot be any national religion. And since public schools are open to children of all religions, these people believe there shouldn't be any religious activities in these schools. Basically, the courts have said that students can pray at school privately, but they can't do it during class time, and the school or the teachers cannot organize or encourage any kind of religious activity.

So to conclude what I've been saying, the freedoms promised in the First Amendment can be very controversial. However, freedom of speech is a basic right guaranteed by the Constitution.

Unit 2: A Diverse Nation
Chapter 3: The Origins of Diversity

Lecture:
"Immigrants to America: Challenges and Contributions"

Before the Lecture:
Listening for transitional phrases that introduce supporting details, pg. 55

1. The four major groups that immigrated to the U.S. during this time were Germans, Irish, Jews from eastern Europe, and Italians. Of course, there were many other immigrants – for instance, from Greece, Hungary, China, and Mexico.

2. Some Americans were worried about the size and diversity of the new foreign population. You have to remember that millions of immigrants arrived during this time, in fact, almost 30 million of them.

3. Most people in the United States were Protestants, and they were often prejudiced against Catholics and also against Jews. One reason for this was that the immigrants' religious practices and traditions seemed strange to them.

4. The Irish, on the other hand, helped build the infrastructure of many American cities – in other words, the canals, the bridges, the railroads, the seaports, and the roads.

Lecture Part 1:
"Immigrants Face Challenges"
Using telegraphic language, pg. 57

Good morning, everyone. Today I want to talk to you about the experience of immigrants who came to the United States from the middle of the nineteenth to the beginning of the twentieth centuries, from, oh, about 1840 to about 1917. Now as you know, there was some strong prejudice against these early immigrants, but even so, these groups were able to make important and lasting contributions to American society. So, for the next few minutes I'm going to discuss both of these parts of the immigrant experience: the prejudice as well as the contributions.

Now just to remind you, the four major groups that immigrated to the U.S. during this time were Germans, Irish, Jews from eastern Europe, and Italians. Of course, there were many other immigrants – for instance, from Greece, Hungary, China, and Mexico. Many of them met with prejudice in this country. Some Americans called them cruel names or mistreated them. Sometimes they refused to rent apartments to immigrants or give them jobs. So now, what were some of the reasons for this?

Well, to begin with, some Americans were worried about the size and diversity of the new foreign population. You have to remember that millions of immigrants arrived during this time, in fact, almost 30 million of them. And most of them crowded into cities in the eastern and northern parts of the United States. I'm sure it was frightening for many Americans to see so many strangers moving into their cities. But there were other reasons for the prejudice against immigrants, too.

Many immigrants faced prejudice because they had different religious beliefs. Most people in the United States were Protestants, and they were often prejudiced against Catholics and also against Jews. One reason for this was that the immigrants' religious practices and traditions seemed strange to them. Then, third, there was prejudice against new immigrants who spoke different languages and had unfamiliar customs: different foods, different clothes, things like that. Also, many Americans were afraid that the immigrants wouldn't share their democratic values. For example, there was a lot of prejudice against the Germans around the time of the First World War because the United States was fighting against Germany, and people thought Germans living in America might be unpatriotic.

And finally, many Americans were afraid that with all these immigrants coming over, they would lose their jobs . . . that the immigrants would work for less money than they would. And so, for all these reasons, immigrants were seen as a threat to the American way of life.

Lecture Part 2:
"Immigrants Make Contributions"
Organizing your notes in columns, pg. 59

What you have to remember is that this time . . . well, it was a time of great expansion in America. Cities and industries were growing, and a lot of people were moving west, so the country needed a large number of new workers. A lot of these new workers were immigrants who made many important and lasting contributions to the development of the country.

For example, many Germans became farmers. They were good at farming and made important improvements to U.S. farming methods. In addition, Germans also worked as tailors, bakers, and butchers. The Irish, on the other hand, helped build the infrastructure of many American cities – in other words, the canals, the bridges, the railroads, the seaports, and the roads. Many were skilled workers, like plumbers, and others were unskilled factory workers.

Jews – who as I said before, were mostly from eastern Europe at this time – and Italians – also made important contributions to the nation. For example, as the years went by, many Jews became involved in popular music and entertainment. They were also important to the development of American education and sciences. Many also worked in the clothing industry. The Italians, like the Irish, were important in the construction industry and in the building of roads, canals, bridges, buildings, and railroads.

Immigrants brought languages, foods, music, religions, beliefs, and different lifestyles to the U.S. In the end, there's no doubt that they made important contributions to the economy and culture of the United States.

Chapter 4: Diversity in the United States of Today

Lecture:
"Recent Immigrants and Today's United States"
Before the Lecture:
Listening for definitions, pg. 72

1. Metaphors are figures of speech that help us understand complex ideas. They're a kind of comparison.

2. A melting pot is a large metal pot – a kind of container – that's used for melting things, such as different metals or foods.

3. Of course, a salad is a dish made up of different vegetables that are mixed together.

4. A patchwork quilt is a cover for a bed that's made from pieces of colorful cloth sewn together.

5. A kaleidoscope is a kind of tube that you look through, and if you turn it, you can see complex, changing patterns.

Lecture Part 1:
"Metaphors for American Society"
Reviewing and revising notes, pg. 76

American society today is more diverse and more complex than ever. Over the years, historians and writers have used different metaphors to try to describe this complex American culture. What I'd like to do today is, first, describe four of those metaphors to you, and then, in the second part of the lecture, talk about transnationalism. *Transnationalism* is a word that describes the relationship that recent immigrants continue to have with their home countries.

All right. To begin, let's talk about what a metaphor is. Metaphors are figures of speech that help us understand complex ideas. They're a kind of comparison.

Let's look at our first slide here. This is probably the oldest metaphor for describing American society. It's a melting pot. A melting pot is a large metal pot – a kind of container – that's used for melting things, such as different metals or foods. You put different ingredients in the pot, heat them, and the ingredients all melt together and become something new. The picture you're looking at is of a fondue – that's a dish from Switzerland that has cheese and other ingredients – but it's melted, so the original ingredients disappear, and the result is something new and different. This metaphor became popular at the beginning of the twentieth century. And so, according to this metaphor, all immigrants coming into the U.S. would lose their separate identities and assimilate, or mix with the people who were already here, and everybody would come together to create a new and unique culture. You see?

But one problem with this metaphor is that it doesn't always describe reality, especially today's reality, which is that although some immigrants do assimilate, many of them have a different experience. For example, some groups are not accepted by the larger society, or maybe they don't want to mix in completely. So instead, what happens is that many immigrants keep parts of their own cultural identity. For example, they may continue to speak their own language. They may celebrate their own traditional holidays. They usually marry someone from their own race – their own ethnic group. And they might never say they are American, even if they live here most of their lives.

So, if the melting pot isn't a good metaphor for describing American culture, what is? Let's look at the next slide here: a salad in a salad bowl. Of course, a salad is a dish made up of different vegetables that are mixed together, but in a salad, each ingredient keeps its own color and taste. So this metaphor represents America as a diverse culture made of different races, ethnic groups, cultures, and languages that live together, but each group may keep parts of its own culture. Do you understand what I mean?

Some people prefer other metaphors for America, like the patchwork quilt. A patchwork quilt is a cover for a bed that's made from pieces of colorful cloth sewn together. Some people like this picture of America because it shows that we're all unique but we're all connected, like the pieces of a quilt. And then a fourth metaphor – you see it here – is a kaleidoscope. A kaleidoscope is a kind of tube that you look through, and if you turn it, you can see complex, changing patterns. This is the metaphor I like best because it's very dynamic. What I mean is that it shows America as a beautiful picture – a multiracial, multiethnic, multicultural society that is always changing.

Lecture Part 2: "Transnationalism"
Using bullets to organize your notes, pg. 77

So, today's immigrants often keep parts of their own cultural identity at the same time as they become part of mainstream American society.

Today's immigrants also maintain some kind of relationship with their countries of origin – I mean the countries where they or their parents were born. And the word that's used to describe this relationship is *transnationalism*, which comes from *trans*, meaning "across," and *nationalism*, which is of course related to the word *nation*; so a *transnational* is a person whose experience goes across nations or cultures.

Many immigrants own homes, land, or businesses in their country of origin. For instance, I have a student who's building a vacation home in Colombia, even though he lives in New York. Other examples . . . immigrants may send money to family members in their native countries. They might continue to support sports teams there. They may travel home frequently, and they may even get involved in business or political affairs there. My neighbor, who's Japanese, has a business in Tokyo in addition to his business in the U.S. He travels there at least five or six times a year to take care of it.

Now, why do you think immigrants today have a closer relationship with their home countries than immigrants did in the past? Well, there are different factors that make this possible, like ease of travel and new technology. See, travel is now more convenient and less expensive than it was years ago, so people can go back and forth between the U.S. and their homeland more often. Second, communication technology has obviously advanced a lot, too, so it's easy for people to stay in contact by phone or by Internet. It's also easier to send money to other countries.

So I hope our discussion has helped you see that immigrants today have a complex relationship with their new country, America, as well as their countries of origin.

Unit 3: The Struggle for Equality
Chapter 5: The Struggle Begins

Lecture:
"The Civil Rights Movement and the Women's Movement"

Before the Lecture:
Listening for guiding questions, page 96

1. So, these are just a few examples of important events in the early struggle for civil rights. What happened next? Well, these events led to more protests, more demonstrations, and more sit-ins throughout the '60s.

2. Today we can look back and be thankful for the great achievements of the civil rights movement. What were some of these achievements? Well, first, the Jim Crow laws were overturned.

3. A journalist named Betty Friedan wrote a book called *The Feminine Mystique*. It was based on interviews with white, middle-class women living in the suburbs. And what do you think Friedan discovered? That these women were very unhappy with their lives because of their lack of freedom and their lack of a sense of identity.

4. Was the women's movement successful? In some ways yes, of course. Today "equal pay for equal work" is the law.

Lecture Part 1:
"The Civil Rights Movement"

Creating your own symbols and abbreviations, page 98

The topic of today's lecture is "The Civil Rights Movement and the Women's Movement." Let's see, to begin, let me remind you that the '60s was a time of great and often violent change in the United States. There were many political and social movements. I'm going to be speaking to you about two important movements that not only involved thousands of people all over the nation but also led to new laws that gave us many of the rights we have today.

First, I'm going to talk about the civil rights movement. Do you know about this period in U.S. history? The Civil Rights Movement was the struggle by hundreds of thousands of people working over many years to achieve equal rights for African Americans. You see, almost 100 years after the end of slavery in the United States, segregation and discrimination against blacks was still common. For example, blacks in many states still couldn't eat in the same places as whites. They couldn't swim in the same swimming pools as whites or sit down on a bus if a white person was standing. The anger that black people felt over these unfair conditions is what started the Civil Rights Movement.

It's difficult to point to the year that the movement began, but there were several key historical events. On December 1, 1955, in the city of Montgomery, Alabama, a black woman named Rosa Parks refused to give up her seat to a white person. This led to the famous Montgomery bus boycott. For one year the entire black community refused to ride on the city buses. The bus company lost a great deal of money, and in the end, the Alabama courts ruled that racial segregation on buses was unconstitutional, and the city of Montgomery was forced to change its policy.

A few years later, in 1960, black students in North Carolina refused to leave a restaurant when the owner wouldn't serve them food because of their color. This kind of protest – they – they were called sit-ins because people would sit and refuse to leave – this kind of protest soon spread like fire all over the South. And how many of you have heard of Martin Luther King Jr.? Well, in 1963, there was a huge national demonstration in Washington, D.C., called the March on Washington, where about 200,000 people heard King give his famous "I have a dream" speech.

So these are just a few examples of important events in the early struggle for civil rights. What happened next? Well, these events led to more protests, more demonstrations, and more sit-ins throughout the '60s, with hundreds of thousands of ordinary people, black and white, struggling together to stop prejudice and discrimination.

Today we can look back and be thankful for the great achievements of the civil rights movement. What were some of these achievements? Well, first, the Jim Crow laws were overturned. This meant that segregation became illegal. Second, the federal government passed laws, like the Civil Rights Act of 1964 and the Voting Rights Act of 1965, which guaranteed the rights of black Americans. Finally, and maybe most important of all, the successes of the civil rights movement led other groups to begin fighting for justice and equality.

Lecture Part 2:
"The Women's Movement"
Organizing your notes in a chart, page 100

Now, the women's movement was related in some ways to the civil rights movement, and that's what we'll turn to next. I'm going to tell you about some important events in the history of the movement from the 1940s until today and talk about the movement's main achievements. Now, were you aware that during World War II, when thousands of men were fighting in Europe and Asia, women took over the men's jobs? They worked in factories, in construction, in offices – anywhere they were needed. However, in 1945, when the men returned from the war, the women had to leave many of those jobs and go back home, back to their roles as wives and mothers. But by the 1950s, more and more women were feeling dissatisfied with these roles.

You see, although about 30 percent of women worked outside the home, they were often paid much less, less than half of what men earned, even if they were doing the same job. Plus, women didn't have the same opportunities as men. They could be teachers or nurses or secretaries. The few women working in business had almost no chance to become managers or executives even if they were qualified and worked hard.

Then, in 1963, a journalist named Betty Friedan wrote a book called *The Feminine Mystique*. It was based on interviews with white, middle-class women living in the suburbs, and what do you think Friedan

discovered? That these women were very unhappy with their lives because of their lack of freedom and their lack of a sense of identity. This book shocked America. It became a huge best seller, and nowadays, looking back, we can say it marked the beginning of the modern women's movement.

Starting in the mid-1960s, after *The Feminine Mystique* came out, women began to organize and work hard for equal opportunity. They marched in the streets, they tried to elect more women to Congress, they gave speeches, and they wrote letters. They demanded equal opportunities for women in education and at work. They asked, "Why shouldn't women be able to be doctors, lawyers, business professionals, as well as police officers, firefighters, and construction workers?" Of course, these were professions that women didn't traditionally do. But they didn't stop there. Another one of their key demands was "equal pay for equal work."

So looking back, was the women's movement successful? In some ways, yes, of course. Today "equal pay for equal work" is the law. More women than men go to college these days. More students in medical school are women than men. There are women politicians, women on the Supreme Court, and women who are university presidents. It is certainly true that women today have more control over their lives than they did 50 years ago. But we still have work to do. For example, women today still earn only about 80 cents for every dollar that a man earns, and if a woman has a baby, she often risks her job. So we've made great progress, but inequalities still exist.

Chapter 6: The Struggle Continues

Lecture:
"Two Important Laws in the Struggle for Equality"

Before the Lecture:
Listening for signal words and phrases, page 115

1. Now to refresh your memory, the '60s was an important decade because during this time, several important laws gave more rights to women, African Americans, and immigrants.

2. Let's begin with the first one, the Age Discrimination Act. I think we need to talk about first, the reasons why this law was needed; second, what it does; and third, well, its impact.

3. Before this law, employers could set an age limit for job applicants.

4. Well, of course, it refers to hiring and firing. In other words, age can't be used as a reason for refusing to hire an older person.

5. In addition, age can't be used as a reason to promote someone to a better position.

6. The ADA also covers people who face discrimination because they have a serious illness.

7. In terms of mental disabilities, there has been progress, too. Today, some businesses are exploring ways to hire people with mental disabilities if they are capable of doing a particular job – like, well, bagging groceries or greeting customers when they go to a store

8. But I think the most important impact of this law is that it's helped to change the way we think.

9. In many places in the world, people with disabilities have to stay at home because there is no way for them to get around.

Lecture Part 1:
"The Age Discrimination in Employment Act"

Indenting, page 117

Hello, everyone. Now to refresh your memory, the '60s was an important decade because during this time, several important laws gave more rights to women, African Americans, and immigrants. But today I'll talk about two other groups: the elderly – I mean senior citizens – and the disabled. The laws that I'll talk about specifically are the Age Discrimination in Employment Act of 1967 and the Americans with Disabilities Act of 1990.

Let's begin with the first one, the Age Discrimination Act. I think we need to talk about first, the reasons why this law was needed; second, what it does; and third, well, its impact.

So first of all, why did the United States need this law? Well, the law tried to correct several problems, mainly, that older people faced a lot of discrimination in the workplace. Before this law, employers could set an age limit for job applicants. For example, they might say that only applicants under age 35 could apply.

The law tries to change this situation. Basically, it protects people over 40 years old from discrimination at work and it covers a lot of areas. Well, of course, it refers to hiring and firing. In other words, age can't be used as a reason for refusing to hire an older person, and employers cannot fire older people because of their age, either. In addition, age can't be used as a reason to promote someone to a better position or give them particular jobs.

The impact of this law has been quite significant. If you're applying for a job nowadays, you won't see anything about age on an application. And a second example is that older workers can get the same benefits as younger people – health insurance, and so on. Also, in most cases, mandatory retirement is not allowed nowadays. In other words, your company cannot force you to retire. You might ask: Do employers actually follow this law? Well, there are still many thousands of legal complaints about age discrimination each year, so we have to be realistic about this. There is still some discrimination against older workers. For example, a recent study showed that companies are more than 40 percent more likely to interview a younger job applicant than an older job applicant. However, people are definitely more aware of age discrimination than they were before.

Lecture Part 2:
"The Americans with Disabilities Act"
Using an outline, page 119

Now let's turn to the second law – the Americans with Disabilities Act, which is often called the ADA for short. This law was passed in 1990, and it protects people with disabilities against discrimination in different places, for example, at work, in housing, and in education.

By "disability" we mean first, any physical or mental condition that limits a person's ability to participate in a major life activity like walking, seeing, or hearing. The ADA also covers people who face discrimination because they have a serious illness. It covers both physical and mental disabilities.

Let me describe the impact of the ADA. This law has changed life for thousands of disabled people across the country. If you've ridden a public bus in an American city, for example, you know that they all have special mechanisms to help people in wheelchairs get on and off the bus. And doorways have to be wide for the same reason – so that people in wheelchairs can easily get in and out of buildings.

In terms of mental disabilities, there's been progress, too. Today, some businesses are exploring ways to hire people with mental disabilities if they are capable of doing a particular job – like, well, bagging groceries or greeting customers when they go to a store. And students with learning difficulties can get help, such as extra time on tests.

But I think the most important impact of this law is that it's helped to change the way we think. In many places in the world, people with disabilities have to stay at home because there is no way for them to get around, and they are also often rejected by society. We need to understand that having a disability doesn't mean people can't participate in society, and people with particular disabilities can do many things to help them lead happy and productive lives. In 1990, when President George H. W. Bush signed the Americans with Disabilities Act into law, he said, "Let the shameful wall of exclusion finally come tumbling down." In other words, that the wall that had always separated disabled people from everyone else should disappear. Respect is the key here. What this means is that our goal needs to be inclusion – equality and full participation for all people, including people with disabilities.

Unit 4: American Values
Chapter 7: American Values from the Past

Lecture:
"Three American Folk Heroes"

Before the Lecture:
Listening for key words, page 138

1. Today I'm going to talk about three traditional American folk heroes. And by folk heroes, I mean real people or imaginary figures who do extraordinary things or who have extraordinary powers.

2. So let's begin with the cowboy. Think about all the places you see cowboys. If you turn on the TV, I guarantee you'll find a cowboy movie on one of the channels. And the image of the cowboy is also seen constantly in advertising and in fashion.

3. An entrepreneur is a person who starts a company – who makes business deals in order to make a profit. We think of entrepreneurs as people who have great ideas and take risks. And the entrepreneur is also a very powerful symbol of American values.

4. There are all kinds of superheroes – Superman, Batman, Wonder Woman, and so on. Most superheroes have extraordinary powers, even though they are in some ways very human.

Lecture Part 1:
"Cowboys and Entrepreneurs"

Clarifying your notes, page 140

Good afternoon, everyone. Today I'm going to talk about three traditional American folk heroes. And by folk heroes, I mean real people or imaginary figures who do extraordinary things or who have extraordinary powers. The United States, like every country, has many of these traditional folk heroes, but I want to talk about three famous ones, and they are the cowboy, the entrepreneur, and the superhero. In this country, we see these three images everywhere – in the media, in advertising. . . . They represent some of our most important values, and I think that's why they're so popular.

So, let's begin with the cowboy. Think about all the places you see cowboys. If you turn on the TV, I guarantee you'll find a cowboy movie on one of the channels. And the image of the cowboy is also seen constantly in advertising and in fashion. In fact, I bet that 90 percent of the people in this room are probably wearing jeans.

Why do you think the cowboy is such a popular image in our culture? Well, let's go back in history about 150 years. During the nineteenth century, people began moving west in order to make their fortune. Some of these settlers started large cattle ranches and hired cowboys. Over time the cowboy became a classic American hero. Think about it: The cowboy works alone, in difficult weather and dangerous conditions. He is completely self-reliant. He never seems to need money or anything like that! He represents courage, freedom, and independence – qualities that almost all Americans still value today.

OK, so next, let's go on to talk about the entrepreneur. An entrepreneur is a person who starts a company – who makes business deals in order to make a profit. We think of entrepreneurs as people who have great ideas and take risks. And the entrepreneur is also a very powerful symbol of American values. That's because entrepreneurs represent the idea that if you're smart, if you work hard, and if you have good ideas, you can succeed. This kind of success story has been popular ever since the Horatio Alger stories of the early twentieth century. And although many young Americans have never heard of Horatio Alger, they certainly know of Steve Jobs or other successful people who have become American heroes because of their talent, their belief in themselves, and the risks that they take.

Now, the last American hero I'd like you to think about is imaginary. I'm talking about the kind of superhero found in comic books, movies, and television. There are all kinds of superheroes: Superman, Batman, Wonder Woman, and so on. Most superheroes have extraordinary powers even though they are in some ways very human.

Superheroes appeal to our deepest fantasies and desires. They're fast and they're powerful, but they have a strong sense of right and wrong. Superman, for example, is always defending the good guys and punishing the bad guys. Most Americans relate very strongly to the values that the superhero represents, and that's why they are so popular in our culture.

Lecture Part 2: "Questions and Answers"

Taking notes on questions and answers, page 141

Lecturer: All right, are there any questions?

Student: Professor Peterson, can you explain a little more about entrepreneurs? Are they always very successful?

Lecturer: Well, some of them aren't successful; others are. But after the Civil War, there was a period of huge industrial expansion in the United States. Thousands of miles of railroads were built and that made it possible for industries like steel and oil to grow. And since that time there have been some entrepreneurs who have been very, very successful and become extremely rich. Have you heard of, uh, let's see, Andrew Carnegie? He made millions of dollars from his steel factories. Oh, and I bet you've heard of John D. Rockefeller. He made his fortune in oil. Carnegie and Rockefeller were two of our earliest entrepreneur-heroes. Another question?

Student: Are there any more modern entrepreneurs that have this "hero quality" you've been describing?

Lecturer: Sure! A couple people come to mind. In addition to Steve Jobs, the brilliant CEO of Apple, I can think of Bill Gates, the co-founder of Microsoft, and Mark Zuckerberg, the Internet entrepreneur. The most amazing thing is that these men all exemplify a lot of the values we've already spoken about. They're seen as people who have the personal qualities that guarantee success.

Student: I'm really interested in where these values come from, so can you talk a bit more about Superman? Did the Superman figure come out in the nineteenth century?

Lecturer: No, the first Superman comic book was written a little later, in the 1930s, and the other superhero characters came after that. One after another after another! Have you seen X-Men or Batman? They come out with one sequel after the other. Movies about superheroes are some of the most profitable movies in history! It seems like Americans never get tired of the superhero image. Incidentally, let's not forget the James Bond films. They're British, of course, but they've been coming out since the 1960s, and they also communicate similar values.

Student: Professor, I have a question. You didn't mention almost any women folk heroes. Why not?

Lecturer: Well, yes, I thought about that. The thing is, there are very few traditional folk heroes who are women. There was a woman named Annie Oakley in the nineteenth century who was famous for her shooting skills. At a time when most women were wives and mothers, she traveled around and had shooting competitions with men. Also, she gave a lot of the money she made to different charities. And then there's Wonder Woman, as I said before, the comic book superhero. She first appeared in 1941. But most of the traditional folk heroes have been men, although I would hope that's going to change in the future.

Chapter 8: American Values Today

Lecture: "Conservative and Liberal Values in American Politics"

Before the Lecture:
Listening for general statements, page 156

1. But even though people's values are very diverse, the strongest voices in American politics today do generally fall into two groups: conservative and liberal.

2. Conservatives usually put a strong emphasis on personal responsibility.

3. Most liberals, on the other hand, think the government should be very active in fixing social problems like poverty and illness.

4. Generally, conservatives think government is too big and expensive.

5. Conservatives typically believe the government

should stay out of the way of business.

6. But in general, liberals believe that government should control and regulate business through strict laws or taxes.

Lecture Part 1:
"Conservative and Liberal Values"

Taking notes in a point-by-point format, page 157

Good morning, everyone. The focus today will be conservative and liberal values in American politics. Of course, you have to understand that I can only talk about these things in a general way today, because this is a very broad topic. It's very hard to make specific statements about Americans' political beliefs since there are more than 300 million Americans from so many different racial, religious, and economic backgrounds. But even though people's values are very diverse, the strongest voices in American politics today do generally fall into two groups: conservative and liberal. So let me outline for you some of the basic differences between conservatives and liberals in three areas: the role of government, taxes, and government regulation of business.

Let's begin with the role of government. Conservatives usually put a strong emphasis on personal responsibility. They think that people should be responsible for themselves. In other words, they don't believe it's the government's responsibility to pay for social programs that guarantee things like a minimum wage or health insurance. Most liberals, on the other hand, think the government should be very active in fixing social problems like poverty and illness. Liberals believe it's the responsibility of the government to provide money and help for people who are poor or sick. So for example, they typically support laws that guarantee workers a minimum wage or free lunches at school for poor children.

Now let's move to the second difference I wanted to mention. Generally, conservatives think government is too big and expensive. A big government requires citizens to pay high taxes to support its programs. And, high taxes are not popular with conservatives, especially during economic recessions. Conservatives are in favor of cutting taxes for the rich as a way of stimulating job creation and economic growth. But liberals believe taxes are necessary because they help government provide the services we need, uh, for an equal and productive society. Taxes are important because they give government money to support social programs like the ones I mentioned before. OK?

Finally, conservatives typically believe the government should stay out of the way of business, that it shouldn't interfere too much in the way business works. They think that an economy with less government control is the best way for the economy to grow and to provide jobs. But in general, liberals believe that government should control and regulate business through strict laws or taxes, because if it doesn't, they think entrepreneurs won't care about their workers, their customers, or the environment. They'll only care about their own profits. So, many liberals think business should be closely regulated, and they favor establishing government programs as a way of stimulating employment opportunities during economic recessions.

Lecture Part 2:

"Values and Political Parties"

Using information on the board to help you take notes, page 159

Let me remind you that the U.S. has two main political parties, so in an election, voters generally choose between the Republicans and the Democrats. And in general I think most people associate the Republican Party with conservative values and ideas, and the Democratic Party with liberal ones. But people's values can change over time, and we can see this clearly if we look at the results of the presidential elections of 1964, 1980, 2000, and 2008.

Can you all see the board? What you'll notice immediately is that there has been a noticeable change in the voting patterns over the past 40-something years. In 1964, a majority of votes – about 61 percent – were for the Democratic candidate for president, Lyndon Johnson. Sixteen years later, in 1980, more than 50 percent of the votes went to the Republican candidate, Ronald Reagan. Reagan won by nearly 60 percent when he ran for a second term four years later. In 2000, the voters were more equally divided. In fact, the country was split down the middle – about half voted for Republican candidate George W. Bush, and half for the Democratic candidate, Al Gore. In the end, the Republicans won that year, but the results were very, very close. Then in 2008, the Democratic Party again won the national elections, with 53 percent of the vote. The situation in 2012 was similar. In that election, Barack Obama won his reelection campaign, but only by the slimmest of margins.

Why do changes like these happen? How do we explain them? Well, sometimes changes in voting patterns are the result of economic conditions, meaning, for example, that voters are responding to high employment or unemployment rates. A strong economy helped Ronald Reagan get elected for a second term in 1984, for example. Or, there could be other reasons, such as concern about the international situation. The attack of September 11, 2001, was probably a factor in George W. Bush's reelection in 2004. But obviously, a third reason for changing voting patterns is that a new generation of voters have different values from the generation that came before them. Millennials don't necessarily vote the same way as their parents, the Baby Boomers. And people's values often change as they get older and they tend to become more conservative. On the other hand, as more young people participate in elections, the strength of the Democratic Party tends to increase. This was evident in 2008 in the election of Barack Obama.

I want to emphasize that I've been discussing American political values and the political system in a very general way. In practice, many Americans are not strict conservatives or liberals; they may have conservative beliefs on some issues and liberal ideas on others. And all Democrats and Republicans are not the same, either. You know, often we see our country divided on the map between red and blue states. But in my opinion, all 50 states are actually different shades of purple because there are both conservative and liberal voters in every state in the nation.

Appendix

Academic Word List vocabulary

achieve
achievement
adapt
adaptation
appropriate
authority
authorized
aware
benefit
boycott
challenge
challenging
comment
communicate
communication
complex
complexity
conclusion
constant
contribute
contribution
controversy
controversial
cooperate
create
creation
creativity
culture
cultural
demonstrate
demonstration
discriminate

discrimination
diverse
diversity
dramatic
economic
economy
emphasize
energetic
energy
environment
environmental
ethnic
ethnicity
eventually
expanded
expansion
foundation
founding
generation
goal
identification
identify
identity
impact
incidentally
interpret
interpretation
individual
involve
involvement
legal
legality

minimum
inconclusive
obvious
obviously
participate
participation
positive
professional
professionally
promote
publish
react
reaction
required
requirement
respond
segregation
significant
similarity
similarly
specific
survival
survive
symbol
symbolize
team
tradition
traditional
traditionally
unidentified
unique
uniquely

Skills Index

Credits

The authors and publishers acknowledge the following sources of copyright material and are grateful for the permissions granted. While every effort has been made, it has not always been possible to identify the sources of all the material used, or to trace all copyright holders. If any omissions are brought to our notice, we will be happy to include the appropriate acknowledgements on reprinting.

Text Credits

Page 110: 'Walls: A Poem for Tolerance' by Pebbles Salas.

Illustration Credits

Page 7, 45, 47, 64, 74, 77, 88: Kamae Design

Page 27: Cartoon from 'The New Yorker Collection', by Robert Mankoff, 1992, www.cartoonbank.com.

Page 112: Tom Croft

Photography Credits

1 ©Junius Brutus Stearns/Bettmann/Corbis; 3 (*right*) ©Stefano Bianchetti/Fine Art/Corbis; (*left*) ©Andrew B. Graham/The Gallery Collection/Fine Art Premium/Corbis; (*background*) ©Jeremy Edwards/iStockphoto; 4 ©Jeremy Edwards/iStockphoto; 5 ©Joseph Sohm; Visions of America/Encyclopedia/Corbis; 6 ©Hill Street Studios/Blend Images/Corbis; 18 (*left to right*) ©MLADEN ANTONOV/AFP/Getty Images; ©TIM SLOAN/AFP/Getty Images; ©Leslie E. Kossoff/Pool/Corbis News/Corbis; 26 ©Olga Paslawska/E+/Getty Images; 28 ©iStockphoto/Thinkstock; 29 (*top to bottom*) ©Photo and Co/The Image Bank/Getty Images; ©George Frey/Bloomberg via Getty Images/Getty Images; 39 (*FD Roosevelt*) ©PoodlesRock/Fine Art/Corbis; (*Jackson*) ©Universal Images Group/Superstock; (*Jefferson*) ©Superstock; (*Kennedy*) ©Superstock; (*Lincoln*) ©Library of Congress/Science Faction/Superstock; (*Madison*) ©Universal Images Group/Superstock; (*Eisenhower*) ©ClassicStock.com/Superstock; (*Washington*) ©Universal Images Group/Superstock; (*Wilson*) ©Image Asset Management Ltd./Superstock; (*T Roosevelt*) ©Classic Vision/age fotostock/Superstock; (*Obama*) ©Pete Souza/Obama Transition Office via Getty Images/Getty Images; 41 ©Ryan McVay/Stone+/Getty Images; 43 ©The Art Archive/Alamy; 49 ©Library of Congress; 52 (*left to right*) ©Interim Archives/Getty Images; ©philipus/Alamy; 58 ©Bettmann/Corbis; 61 ©Library of Congress; 62 ©Kevork Djansezian/Getty Images; 69 ©DNY59/iStockphoto; 70 ©Bebeto Matthews/Corbis; 71 (*left to right*) ©Oleg Belov/Shutterstock; ©Africa Studio/Shutterstock; ©John Warden/Superstock; ©Philippe Regard/Lifesize/Getty Images; 75 (*top to bottom*) ©Oleg Belov/Shutterstock; ©Africa Studio/Shutterstock; ©John Warden/Superstock; ©Dennis Degnan/Cusp/Corbis; 83 ©Hulton Archive/Getty Images; 85 ©New York Times Co./Archive Photos/Getty Images; 87 (*top to bottom*) ©Susan Law Cain/Shutterstock; 87 ©Buyenlarge/Archive Photos/Getty Images; 87 ©Paul Thompson/Hulton Archive/Getty Images; ©PhotoQuest/Archive Photos/Getty Images; 93 (*left to right*) ©Bettmann/Corbis; ©Stock Montage/Archive Photos/Getty Images; ©Consolidated News Pictures/Hulton Archive/Getty Images; 94 (*clockwise from left to right*) ©Jose CABEZAS/AFP/Getty Images; ©Marka/Superstock; ©Bettmann/Corbis; ©Bettmann/Corbis; ©Popperfoto/Getty Images; ©Historical/Corbis; 98 ©Hulton Archive/Archive Photos/Getty Images; 102 ©MN Chan/Getty Images News/Getty Images; 104 ©Ivan Solis/iStockphoto; 105 ©Ron Bailey/iStockphoto; 108 (*clockwise from left to right*) ©iStockphoto/Thinkstock; ©alle12/iStockphoto; ©cromic/Shutterstock; ©Jill Fromer/iStockphoto; ©sagir/Shutterstock; 111 ©Image Source/Superstock; 114 (*clockwise from left to right*) ©Najlah Feanny/Corbis News/Corbis; ©Masterfile; ©Masterfile; ©Rubberball/iStockphoto; 116 ©Jetta Productions/Iconica/Getty Images; 123 ©Historical/Corbis; 125 ©Ron Sherman/Stone/Getty Images; 127 ©Bettmann/Corbis; 128 ©Horatio Alger, Wait and Hope, 2004. By permission of Pavilion Press/By Permission of Pavilion Press; 129 ©ColorBlind Images/Blend Images/Getty Images; 137 (*left to right*) ©Kim Kulish/Corbis News/Corbis; ©Robert Dale/Images.com/Corbis; ©Masterfile; 141 ©Bettmann/Corbis; 143 ©John Henley/keepsake RM/Corbis; 145 (*left to right*) ©Dougal Waters/Digital Vision/Getty Images; ©MGP/Photodisc/Getty Images; ©Jupiterimages/Brand X Pictures/Thinkstock; 146 ©CREATISTA/Shutterstock